# The Origin of Rights

by

## The Honourable Roger E. Salhany

CARSWELL
Toronto • Calgary • Vancouver
1986

**Canadian Cataloguing in Publication Data**

Salhany, Roger E.
The origin of rights

Bibliography: p.
Includes index.
ISBN 0-459-38750-2 (bound). — ISBN 0-459-38760-X (pbk.)

1. Civil rights — Canada — History.  2. Civil
rights — United States — History.  3. Civil
rights — Great Britain — History.  I. Title.

K3240.4.S34 1986        342.085′09        C86-093741-0


© 1986 by The Carswell Company Limited

To my children
who make every day
an adventure

# Preface

Too many Canadians take their freedoms for granted — as if they have always been a concomitant of our evolutionary growth. But any historian knows that this is just not so. Our rights and freedoms were the results of years of struggles by individuals and groups. And more often than not, those who struggled hardest and fought longest — and suffered the most — were not prime ministers, generals and judges. They were persons who were regarded as misfits and outcasts by their contemporaries. This book is about them — how their unwavering belief in their cause forged those liberties which Canadians decided on April 17, 1982 to enshrine in the Charter of Rights and Freedoms.

This book is not a textbook. It was never intended to be. It all started when an interest in legal history, which was first stimulated as a graduate law student at Cambridge University in the early '60s, was rekindled by the advent of the Charter. To complete the picture, it was only natural to turn to American sources to discover how their Bill of Rights originated and developed. It became obvious to me that no one could really understand our liberties today unless they were viewed in perspective — the era that spawned them. As I did my research it suddenly dawned on me that members of the legal profession and the public might also find their history as fascinating as I did.

I was fortunate enough to be able to call upon my colleagues Janet Scott, Bud Wong and Sam Filer for their critical comments and was delighted to also receive their helpful encouragement. But I am particularly grateful to Mrs. Irene Parker who generously typed the material in her spare time and prodded me along when my energy waned.

March 24, 1986                                      Roger Salhany
                                                   New Dundee

# Contents

# 1

# The Quest for a Charter of Rights and Freedoms

Our liberty is not Caesar's. It is a blessing we have received from God himself. It is what we are born to. To lay this down at Caesar's feet, which we derive not from him, which we are not beholden to him for, were an unworthy action, and a degrading of our very nature.

John Milton, Defence of the People of England (1651)

Wherever the real power in a Government lies, there is danger of oppression. In our Governments the real power lies in the majority of the community, and the invasion of private rights is chiefly to be apprehended, not from acts of Government contrary to the sense of its constituents, but from acts in which the Government is the mere instrument of the major number of the constituents ... Wherever there is an interest and power to do wrong, wrong will generally be done, and not less readily by a powerful and interested party than by a powerful and interested prince.

James Madison in a letter to Thomas Jefferson,
October 17, 1788

Government of limited power need not be anemic government. Assurance that rights are secure tends to diminish fear and jealousy of strong government, and by making us feel safe to live under it makes for its better support. Without promise of a limiting Bill of Rights it is doubtful if our Constitution could have mustered enough strength to enable its ratification. To enforce these rights today is not to choose weak government over strong government. It is only to adhere as a means of strength to individual freedom of mind in preference to officially disciplined uniformity, for which history indicates a disappointing and disastrous end.

Mr. Justice Jackson, *West Virginia State Board of Education v. Barnette* (1943)

On April 17, 1982, Queen Elizabeth II proclaimed the Constitution Act before a rain soaked crowd of 30,000 people on Parliament Hill in Ottawa. Across the nation another million Canadians watched the ceremony with pride in their homes, in restaurants, in social clubs and in neighbourhood taverns. Canadians had finally come of age. Canadians now had their own constitution — not one fashioned in a foreign land by an impersonal government and subject, theoretically, to amendment without consulting the Canadian Government — but one made in Canada designed to fulfill Canadian aspirations.

More important, Canadians now had a Charter of Rights and Freedoms, modelled somewhat after the American Bill of Rights. Of course, not everyone then, or today, felt that we needed a Charter of Rights and Freedoms to protect us from government intrusion. Was not government itself merely the elected representatives of every Canadian chosen to represent the views of the majority of Canadians? Was not the very concept of a Charter of Rights and Freedoms or a Bill of Rights inconsistent with the concept of supremacy of Parliament? To understand the events leading up to the proclamation, it is necessary to turn back the pages of history several centuries.

## Parliament Struggles for Supremacy

The five centuries which span the beginning of the House of Normandy, starting with the conquest of William I in 1066 and ending with the last Tudor, Elizabeth I, was a period during which supreme authority was vested in the reigning sovereign. Although most English Kings, and Elizabeth I, had difficulty in raising the funds needed to carry out their wars and often had to turn to both nobles and later parliament for money, this rarely prevented them from exercising their absolute authority. That authority was believed to flow from God and was subject, only, to the natural law. As Bracton wrote:

> There are also under the king the freemen and serfs subject to his power, and every person is under him, and he is under no person but is only under God. . . . But the king himself ought not to be subject to man, but subject to God and to the law, for the law makes the king.

The ascension of the House of Stuart signalled the end of the belief that kings were divinely ordained to rule and that their royal prerogative was unassailable. James I quarrelled frequently with his Parliament. His son, Charles I, decided to rule without Parliament for 11 years. In the end, he succumbed to the need to raise funds to pay for a war with Scotland and reconvened Parliament. So badly was Charles in need of money that he was forced to concede to Parliament almost everything that it sought. When he later attempted to revoke his concessions and assume control over the army, he lost his head and Parliament was eventually victorious. Charles's two sons Charles II and James II, restored after the Commonwealth, were able to make their compromises with Parliament but by this time it was clear that the supremacy of Parliament prevailed.

To many Englishmen, the supremacy of Parliament was now little more than the exchange of one form of absolutism for another. In 1645, during the reign of Charles I, the first political party in England known as the Levellers (derisively called because they wished to level men's estates) originated. They demanded that if there was to be genuine representative democracy, real sovereignty should be transferred to the House of Commons, that there should be a wider redistribution of seats and annual parliaments. They also advanced a programme of economic reform in the interests of small tradesmen, artisans and farmers, and advocated freedom of religious worship and organization. They believed that all people possessed inalienable rights conferred on them not by Parliament but by God. These rights were embodied in a written constitution called the Agreement of the People, which the Levellers presented to the public. England, however, was not ready for such a radical change to its institutions and rejected the Agreement.

## A Bill of Rights is Born

The idea of a constitution which safeguarded fundamental inalienable rights against raw parliamentary power was carried to the American colonies. But even the delegates to the Federal Convention of 1787 did not feel that a Bill of Rights was a necessary adjunct to the Constitution. Some, such as Alexander Hamilton of New York insisted that a Bill of Rights historically had no place in a Constitution which recognized that sovereignty resided with the people. Since the people surrendered nothing to the government organized under the Constitution, it was not necessary for the people to reserve to themselves anything in particular. The danger with a Bill of Rights, he argued, was that if the Constitution contained a list of rights to be protected, some might be inadvertently overlooked. This omission would give the government the pretext of saying that those rights were expressly abandoned to the government.

Thomas Jefferson, who had been instrumental in drafting the Declaration of Independence, but had not been a member of the constitutional convention, argued eloquently for a Bill of Rights. In a letter to James Madison which he wrote from Paris on December 20, 1787, he stressed that "a bill of rights is what the people are entitled to against every government on earth, general or particular; and what no just government should refuse, or rest on inference." In another letter written to Madison on March 15, 1789, he expressed his view that "the tyranny of the legislatures is the most formidable dread at the present, and will be for many years."

It was largely through the efforts of James Madison that a Bill of Rights was eventually adopted by the House of Representatives at the First Congress. During the summer of 1789, Madison and 10 members of a congressional committee drafted a Bill of Rights containing 10 amendments to the Constitution. These were approved in 1791 by the House of Representatives and the Senate.

Although the 10 amendments constituting the first Bill of Rights were eventually ratified by all of the States of the Union, it took almost 50 years for the Supreme Court of the United States to decide that the restraints upon government listed in the 10 amendments were only upon the federal government and not the state government. In the landmark decision *Barron v. The Mayor and City Council of Baltimore,* Chief Justice Marshall of the Supreme Court of the United States explained:

> The constitution was ordained and established by the people of the United States for themselves, for their own government, and not for the government of the individual states. Each state established a constitution for itself, and, in that constitution, provided such limitations and restrictions on the powers of its particular government as its judgment dictated. . . . (The Bill of Rights and the provisions of the Constitution) are limitations of power granted in the instrument itself; not of distinct governments, framed by different persons and for different purposes.

It took another 30 years and the American Civil War to impose limitations upon state authority. After the defeat of the South, Congress passed the Civil Rights Act of 1866 giving "such citizens, of every race and color, without regard to any previous condition of slavery or involuntary servitude . . . to full and equal benefit of all laws and proceedings for the security of person and property, as is enjoyed by white citizens." However, there was concern by northern representatives of Congress that once the southern states were readmitted into the union, they would pass legislation restricting the rights of the negroes for whom a war had just been fought. To give constitutional support to the rights which had caused a civil war, the Fourteenth Amendment to the Constitution was proposed and passed by Congress in 1866. Section 1 provides:

> All persons born or naturalized in the United States, and subject to the jurisdiction thereof, are citizens of the United States and of the State wherein they reside. No State shall make or enforce any law which shall abridge the privileges or immunities of citizens of the United States; nor shall any State deprive any person of life, liberty, or property, without due process of law; nor deny to any person within its jurisdiction the equal protection of the laws.

Over the last century, the Supreme Court of the United States has spent the largest part of its time concerned with the question of the meaning of the Fourteenth Amendment and, in particular, the words "nor shall any State deprive any person of life, liberty, or property, without due process of law." Three views have emerged.

One strongly urged by Justice Hugo Black, during his long tenure on the bench from 1937 to 1971, was that the Fourteenth Amendment was intended to incorporate the first 10 amendments so as to make the provisions of these amendments applicable to all of the state laws. Justice Benjamin Cardozo was not prepared to go that far. In 1937, in *Palko v. Connecticut,* he expressed the opinion that certain rights listed in the first 10 amendments were "the very essence of a scheme of ordered liberty" which had to be protected from state action. Included amongst these fundamental rights were such things as freedom of speech, freedom of the press, freedom of religion. But others such as the right to trial by jury and the right to remain silent were not so essential to a free society. As far as he was concerned, "justice would not perish" without them.

During the last 25 years, the Supreme Court of the United States has not demonstrated any intention to accept either the total incorporation theory of Justice Black or the limited incorporation theory of Justice Cardozo, which includes only those rights which are "the very essence of the scheme of ordered liberty." The Court has chosen the middle ground ensuring that the states will not violate most of the rights specified in the first eight amendments and other certain fundamental rights.

## The British North America Act

Steeped in British tradition which revered the concept of the supremacy of parliament, the early provinces of Canada gave little thought to the necessity of a Bill of Rights which would impose any limitations on their legislatures. Moreover, most politicians believed that the enactment of a Bill of Rights would just be a waste of time; subsequent legislatures could simply override the protections listed or abolish them.

The delegates to the Charlottetown Conference, which opened on September 1, 1864, had more on their minds than a Bill of Rights. The Civil War was in progress in the United States and John A. MacDonald could foresee that if the northern states won it, a reconstructed United States would be looking to extend its boundaries, possibly into Canada. Only a confederation of the four existing provinces would have the financial resources and the manpower to extend their dominion to the Pacific Ocean. As far as MacDonald was concerned, "if Englishmen do not go there, Yankees will." What was needed, he argued, was a strong federal parliament which would have the power and the will to extend Canadian authority from sea to sea.

His colleague in lower Canada, George-Etienne Cartier, was more disturbed that French Canada might be swallowed by its American neighbour. He too wanted a union of the provinces with a central government; however, he felt that French Canada also needed a local legislature to protect its language and heritage.

Maritimers were lukewarm to the idea of union with Canada. It was the age of sailing ships and the provinces were at the height of their prosperity. They preferred to look towards markets abroad rather than markets inland. "Why should our taxes pay for railroads and defence that will benefit Canada and not us?" asked former premier Joseph Howe of Nova Scotia.

The threat of annexation, however, by the United States in April 1865 gave an impetus to the concept of confederation. A further boost came in the spring of 1866 when the Fenians, seeking to foment rebellion against British rule in Ireland, tried to launch an attack against Campobello Island in New Brunswick and captured Fort Erie in June.

Urged on by MacDonald, the English Government pressured the maritime colonies into supporting confederation. On February 12, 1867, the British North America Act was given its first reading in the English House of Lords and passed by that House on February 26. The same day it was introduced into the House of Commons where it received little interest from the members. It finally passed a third reading on March 8 and was given royal assent on March 29, 1867.

The Act itself was concerned mainly with the division of powers between the federal parliament and the provincial legislatures. The provincial legislatures were given exclusive jurisdiction over such local matters as the administration of justice within the province, local works and undertakings, property and civil rights. To the federal parliament was reserved the right to make laws affecting the nation as a whole, e.g., the regulation of trade and commerce, the raising of money by any mode or system of taxation and the criminal law. Furthermore, jurisdiction over matters not exclusively granted to the provinces was reserved to the federal parliament, unlike the American Constitution where it had been given to the states.

Thus, within their exclusive fields of responsibility Parliament and each provincial legislature was supreme. There was no need to enshrine guarantees of individual rights in a Bill of Rights. It was the responsibility of the Parliament of Canada and the provincial legislatures, made up of duly elected representatives of the people, to protect individual rights and freedoms. This had been done in a number of English statutes: the Magna Carta in 1215, the Bill of Rights in 1689 and, finally the Act of Settlement of 1701 which ensured complete independence of the judiciary.

## Canada Chooses a Charter

By the middle of this century, it became evident that Parliament and the provincial legislatures could not be counted upon to protect fundamental freedoms. The most glaring example of this failure occurred in Alberta in 1937 when the Social Credit Government tried to impose censorship on the press to prevent criticism of its attempt to change the provincial banking system.

Since the courts had no Bill of Rights to fall back on, the Supreme Court of Canada turned to the concept of *ultra vires* in determining the constitutional validity of the Bank Taxation Act, the Credit of Alberta Regulation Act and the Accurate News and Information Act. In what became known as the *Alberta Press* case, the Supreme Court of Canada struck down the first two statutes as attempts to regulate banks and banking and trade and commerce, matters that were within the exclusive jurisdiction of the Parliament of Canada. The Accurate News and Information Act, an attempt by the Social Credit Government to censor any criticism of Social Credit policy, was also struck down even though the provinces had exclusive jurisdiction over "property and civil rights", because it was ancillary and dependent upon the first two statutes. Although Chief Justice Duff and Mr. Justice Cannon emphasized that "freedom of discussion" was essential to enlighten public opinion in a democratic state, they conceded that the Parliament of Canada could control free discussion through the use of the criminal law if it chose to do so.

During the latter part of the 1930s and 1940s, the government of the province of Quebec attempted to stifle the efforts of the Jehovah's Witnesses to find new converts by the enactment of the notorious Padlock Law, an Act to Protect the Province against Communist Propaganda. The Act authorized the Quebec Attorney General, who was also the Premier, Maurice Duplessis, to padlock for a period of one year any building suspected of being used for propaganda purposes by communists. This statute as well as municipal by-laws were used to harrass the Witnesses who were considered to be atheists and "the twin brother of communists". In a series of decisions, the Supreme Court of Canada found that the actions of the Quebec Attorney General exceeded the constitutional restrictions of the British North America Act. Out of these decisions, came the first seeds of recognition (in the judgment of Mr. Justice Rand) that there existed an absolute right of freedom of religion.

Until the 1940s, there was little momentum in Canada for a Bill of Rights. The majority of Canadians were content to leave the protection of their rights in the hands of Parliament or their local provincial legislatures. But it was not the majority who had anything to fear. Abroad, Germany had demonstrated how an indifferent majority could allow its government to ruthlessly destroy the lives and crush the liberty of its minorities. In Canada, a government representing the majority of the electors was prepared to ignore the rights of its oriental citizens — the Japanese Canadians.

The first political party to espouse a Bill of Rights in Canada was the C.C.F. party in 1945, moved by their member of Parliament in the House of Commons, Alistair Stuart. The first government to enact a Bill of Rights was the C.C.F. government in Saskatchewan in 1947. In 1946 John Diefenbaker took up the standard and vigorously pursued it until his election as Prime Minister in 1957. The following year he moved the introduction of Bill C-60, a Bill of Rights. After two years of study the Canadian Bill of Rights became a reality and came into force on August 10, 1960.

Unfortunately, the Bill was only an Act of Parliament. Like other statutes passed by that legislative body, it was not constitutionally entrenched and could be amended by a simple majority. Furthermore, it was not binding on any of the provinces. Although the wording of the Bill was similar in many respects to the Charter of Rights and Freedoms, it was considered by the courts more as an instrument assisting in the interpretation of statutes rather than a declaration and guarantee of fundamental rights. Indeed, in the two decades that span the Bill of Rights and the Charter of Rights and Freedoms, there have been only two instances where the Supreme Court of Canada struck down federal legislation because it contravened the Bill of Rights.

The second stage in the development of a Canadian Charter of Rights and Freedoms can be attributed to the appearance of Pierre Elliot Trudeau on the federal political scene. After his appointment in 1967 as Minister of Justice in the government of Prime Minister Lester B. Pearson, Mr. Pearson announced that a Provincial Premiers' Conference would be called to discuss the enshrining of a Bill of Rights. It took, however, another 14 years and several Federal-Provincial Conferences to finally reach an accord. This was achieved in September 1981 with only one province — Quebec — refusing to sign the agreement. On December 2, 1981, Parliament gave the Constitution Act its third and final reading. Six days later, on November 8, 1981 it was passed by the Senate and delivered to the Governor General to be forwarded to Great Britain for passage by the English Parliament and final approval by the Queen.

The Canadian Charter of Rights and Freedoms is not only unique in Canada's constitutional framework, it is totally foreign to the English concept of constitutional monarchy. No longer are Parliament and the provincial legislatures supreme within their own jurisdictional field. Every piece of legislation which they pass must be consistent with the provisions of the Charter otherwise they are of "no force or effect". Section 52 of the Constitution Act admonishes Parliament and the provincial legislatures to recognize that "The Constitution of Canada is the supreme law of Canada".

Section 32(1) of the Charter goes even further. It requires the Government of Canada and of each province to respect the rights and freedoms listed in the Charter. This was pointed out recently by our highest court in *Operation Dismantle Inc. v. The Queen*. Operation Dismantle Inc. and 22 other labour and peace organizations sought an order from the courts prohibiting testing of the cruise missile in Canada on the grounds that it posed a threat to the lives and security of Canadians by increasing the risk of nuclear war. It was argued that by doing so, section 7 of the Charter which guarantees everyone the right to life, liberty and security of the person had been infringed. Counsel for the government argued that the courts had no right to scrutinize and strike down decisions made by the Cabinet.

Chief Justice Dickson of the Supreme Court of Canada disagreed. As far as he was concerned, "the executive branch of the Canadian Government is duty bound to act in accordance with the dictates of the Charter", and the courts were duty bound to ensure that the executive did just that. However, he went on to find that in this case section 7 had not been infringed by the Cabinet because it had not been established there was, in fact, a threat to life and security of Canadian citizens; the allegation was merely based on hypothesis and speculation.

The Charter, on the other hand, does recognize that the rights and freedoms listed in it are not absolute. There may be instances where those rights and freedoms must give way to other interests that are reasonable and can be demonstrably justified. Section 1 of the Charter recognizes that the rights and freedoms listed in it must be,

> [S]ubject only to such reasonable limits prescribed by law as can be demonstrably justified in a free and democratic society.

What are reasonable limits? One can hardly expect them to be detailed in advance. Each can only be assessed and determined in the light of the circumstances under which a particular right or freedom is sought to be curtailed. But what is clear from the section is that the rights and freedoms listed in the Charter are paramount until limits are placed on them by legislation. Those limits must also be "reasonable". They must also be "demonstrably justified" as being reasonable limits which only can be tolerated in a free and democratic society. And it is up to the government to demonstrate that the limits that it wants to impose are reasonable. It is not up to the ordinary citizen to show that the limits upon his rights and freedoms are unreasonable.

In a judgment released by the Supreme Court of Canada on April 24, 1985, *R. v. Big M Drug Mart Ltd.*, Chief Justice Dickson warned that "not every government interest or policy objective" which affected a right or freedom guaranteed by the Charter would be accepted as a reasonable limit.

> Once a sufficiently significant government interest is recognized then it must be decided if the means chosen to achieve this interest are reasonable — a form of proportionality test. The court may wish to ask whether the means adopted to achieve the end sought do so by impairing as little as possible the right or freedom in question.

The rights listed in the Charter are divided into seven categories. They include:

1. fundamental freedoms such as freedom of religion, expression and freedom of the press;

2. democratic rights ensuring that every citizen has the right to vote in an election;
3. mobility rights guaranteeing that every citizen has the right to enter, remain or leave Canada and to move from province to province;
4. legal rights protecting us against unreasonable search and seizure, arbitrary detention and ensuring our right to counsel and that we are presumed innocent until proven guilty;
5. equality rights guaranteeing that every individual regardless of race, religion, sex, age or mental or physical disability is equal before and under the law;
6. ensuring that English and French are the official languages of Canada and requiring their use in Parliament and in the courts; and
7. protecting the rights of citizens whose primary language is French or English to be given education in primary and secondary schools in that language.

Probably the most important and unique section of the Charter is the enforcement section. It prescribes the ways in which the Canadian courts can ensure that the rights or freedoms guaranteed are respected by officials of the state. Other countries which have Charters of Rights and Freedoms do have enforcement sections and therefore it is not for this reason that the Canadian provision is unique. It is unique because the American Bill of Rights has no enforcement section. Canadians have been front row spectators to the struggle which has engaged the Supreme Court of the United States over the past 200 years in their effort to find a satisfactory way of protecting the rights and freedoms of its citizens. Canada has been fortunate to be able to draw on that experience in drafting its own enforcement section.

Since its introduction two years ago, decisions rendered by the courts have received warm support and encouragement in some quarters and harsh criticism in others. Some continue to argue that Canada does not need a Charter of Rights and Freedoms because it will only hamstring the legitimate efforts of the police to suppress crime. It is said that there is a risk that Canadians who have always been law abiding may lose respect for our system of justice. That criticism should remind us of the words of William Pitt over 200 years ago who, in a speech to the House of Commons on November 18, 1783, eloquently urged Englishmen to embrace freedom before necessity.

Necessity is the plea for every infringement of human freedom. It is the argument of tyrants; it is the creed of slaves.

# 2

# Freedom of Conscience and Religion

A government that will coerce its citizens in the domain of the spiritual will hardly hesitate to coerce them in the domain of the temporal. If it will direct how they shall worship it will certainly direct how they shall vote. Certain it is that religious liberty is the progenitor of most other civil liberties. Out of victory in the struggle of freedom to worship as one's conscience dictates come victory in the struggle for freedom to speak as one's reason dictates. Freedom of the press comes from the struggle for freedom to print religious tracts, and freedom to assemble politically can be traced to the successful struggle for freedom to assemble religiously. Even procedural liberties incident to our concept of a fair trial grew largely out of the struggle for procedural fairness in heresy and other religious trials.

Leo Pfeffer, The Liberties of An American,
The Supreme Court Speaks (1963)

The guaranties of civil liberty are but guaranties of freedom of the human mind and spirit and of reasonable freedom and opportunity to express them. They presuppose the right of the individual to hold such opinions as he will and to give them reasonably free expression, and his freedom, and that of the state as well, to teach and persuade others by the communication of ideas. The every essence of the liberty which they guarantee is the freedom of the individual from compulsion as to what he shall think and what he shall say, at least where the compulsion is to bear false witness to his religion. If these guaranties are to have any meaning they must, I think, be deemed to withhold from the state any authority to compel belief or the expression of it where that expression violates religious convictions, whatever may be the legislative view of the desirability of such compulsion.

Mr. Justice Harlan F. Stone,
*Minersville School District v. Gobitis* (1940)

The Jehovah's Witnesses believe that it is not necessary to attain heaven through the grace of the organized Christian churches. Not only have they rejected any attempt to unite with the 20th century ecumenical spirit, they are vocal in their criticisms and attacks on the churches, particularly the Catholic Church. The religious tolerance they demand for themselves is not extended to others. They regard world powers and political parties as the unwitting allies of Satan. It is for this reason that they refuse to take part in public elections or to perform military services or salute the flag of any nation. Founded in Pittsburgh, Pennsylvania in 1872 by Charles Taze Russell, the movement has spread to almost 200 countries and acquired over one million members through a scheme of aggressive door-to-door, person-to-person evangelism and book selling.

In the '30s and early '40s, Quebec, particularly rural Quebec, was still a deeply religious Roman Catholic community. Premier Maurice Duplessis who held a vice-grip on the province, some suggested with the consent of the Church hierarchy, intended to keep it that way. Other forces, however, were working a quiet revolution which would eventually break that vice-grip by the end of the '50s.

It was during this period that the Jehovah's Witnesses decided to invade the province in an effort to discover potential converts. Instead of approaching their task with a measure of tolerance and kindly persuasion, they launched a frontal assault on the Roman Catholic Church and the institutions of that then pastoral province. Although used to door slamming, they were not prepared for the reception awaiting them by the City of Quebec and provincial Premier Duplessis.

On October 27, 1933, the City of Quebec passed By-law 184 which provided that it was,

> forbidden to distribute in the streets of the city of Quebec, any book, pamphlet, booklet, circular, tract whatever without having previously obtained for so doing the written permission of the Chief of Police. (p. 320)

In effect, this by-law required anyone who wanted to distribute any material to appear before the chief of police to obtain his permission. He could agree to permit the material to be distributed or he could refuse. He did not have to give reasons or justify a refusal. There was no appeal from that decision.

Quebec City council said that they had been given authority to pass this by-law by the province of Quebec. The province of Quebec pointed to their powers under section 92(16) of the British North America Act to make laws on "Generally all Matters of a merely local or private Nature in the Province." Even if it did affect the right to freedom of religion, religion was a matter falling within "Property and Civil Rights in the Province," a matter over which the province also had jurisdiction under section 92(13).

Laurier Saumur was a resident of Quebec City and a lawyer. He was also an active Jehovah's Witness who wished to spread his beliefs by their usual methods — that is, meeting people on the streets and going from home to home. According to him, By-law 184 had been expressly adopted to prevent the preachings of the Jehovah's Witnesses; it was arbitrary and discriminatory. There may have been some truth to this. It was passed in 1933, about the time that members of the Jehovah's Witnesses began to appear on the streets of Quebec and were being brought before the courts for various offences. Although other religious groups such as the Seventh Day Adventists had been permitted to sell religious literature from house to house, it was only the Jehovah's Witnesses who were refused.

Saumur brought an application before the Quebec Superior Court for a declaration that the by-law was not authorized by the city of Quebec. The trial was held before Mr. Justice Casgrain of the Quebec Superior Court. Hayden C. Covington, who described himself as an ordained minister of the gospel and a lawyer from Brooklyn, New York, was called by Saumur to give evidence. He was asked to read passages from the publications of the Jehovah's Witnesses and he did so.

> Religion is the adultress and idolatress that befriends and commits religious forni-
> cation with the political and commercial elements. She is the lover of this world and
> blesses the world from the balcony of the Vatican and in the pulpits.

> Religion, whose most powerful representative has ruled from Rome for sixteen
> centuries, traces her origin all the way back to Babylon of Nimrod's founding, and
> organized religion deservedly bears the name Babylon . . .

> I will shew you unto thee the judgment of the great whore (or idolatress) that sitteth
> upon many waters; with whom the kings of the earth have committed fornication, and
> inhabitants of the earth have been made drunk with the wine of her fornication . . .

> full of abominations and filthiness of her fornication; and upon her forehead was a
> name written, MYSTERY, BABYLON THE GREAT, THE MOTHER OF HAR-
> LOTS AND ABOMINATIONS OF THE EARTH.

Mr. Covington was then asked,

> Q. Do you consider that writing such books with such insults against another religion,
> in fact the religion practised by the people of this province or city, proper means of
> preaching the gospel?

> A. I do

He went on to add,

> [H]istory abundantly attests to the fact that the Roman Catholic Church Hierarchy has
> had relationship with the world and has had part tacitly in the wars between the nations
> and the destruction of nations.

A little later he was asked,

> Q. Do you consider necessary for your organization to attack the other religions, in
> fact, the catholic, the protestant and the jews?

> A. Indeed. The reason for this is because the Almighty God commands that errors
> should be exposed and not persons or nations.

He was asked by the trial judge,

> Q. You are the only witnesses of the truth?

A. Jehovah's Witnesses are the only witnesses to the truth of Almighty God Jehovah.

Q. Is the Roman Catholic a true church?

A. No.

Q. Is it an unclean woman?

A. It is pictured in the Bible as a whore, as having illicit relationships with the nations of the world, and history proves that fact, history that all have studied in school.

## Mr. Covington finally added,

If obedience to a law of the state or nation would compel them to thereby violate God's law, they will obey God rather than men. . . .

Q. Notwithstanding the laws of the country to the contrary?

A. Notwithstanding the laws of the country to the contrary.

It is not surprising against this background that Mr. Justice Casgrain dismissed the application of Laurier Saumur to quash the by-law. As far as he was concerned, the by-law was a mere "police" regulation dealing with the maintenance of order and good government in the city and was within the general powers granted by the city charter. The Quebec Court of Appeal agreed and added that the "use of streets" was a subject matter of legislation entirely within provincial jurisdiction. However, a majority of the Supreme Court of Canada could not accept that reasoning. Mr. Justice Rand saw it this way:

What the practice under the by-law demonstrates is that the language comprehends the power of censorship. From its inception, printing has been recognized as an agency of tremendous possibilities, and virtually upon its introduction into western Europe it was brought under the control and licence of government. At that time, as now in despotisms, authority viewed with fear and wrath the uncensored printed word: it is and has been the *bête noire* of dogmatists in every field of thought; and the seed of its legislative control in this country becomes a matter of the highest moment. (p. 326)

He noted that the Christian religion in Europe and in America stood in the first rank of social, political and juristic importance. This was why the people of Quebec were guaranteed their right to practise the Roman Catholic religion by the Articles of Capitulation in 1760, The Treaty of Paris in 1763, and the Quebec Act of 1774. He went on,

From 1760, therefore, to the present moment religious freedom has, in our legal system, been recognized as a principle of fundamental character; and although we have nothing in the nature of an established church, that the untrammelled affirmations of religious belief and its propagation, personal or institutional, remain as of the greatest constitutional significance throughout the Dominion is unquestionable.

He had this to say about the argument that freedom of religion was a matter of civil rights:

That legislation "in relation" to religion and its profession is not a local or private matter would seem to me to be self-evident: the dimensions of this interest are nationwide; it is even today embodied in the highest level of the constitutionalism of Great Britain; it appertains to a boundless field of ideas, beliefs and faiths with the deepest roots and loyalties; a religious incident reverberates from one end of this country to the other, and there is nothing to which the "body politic of the Dominion" is more sensitive.

In his judgment, Mr. Justice Estey added,

The right of the free exercise and enjoyment of religious profession and worship, is a personal, sacred right for which, history records, men have striven and fought. Wherever attained they have resisted restrictions and limitations thereon in every possible manner. In one sense it may be styled a civil right, but it does not follow that it would be included within the phrase "Property and Civil Rights in the Province" within the meaning of s. 92(13) of the *B.N.A. Act.* On the contrary it would rather seem that such a right should be included among those upon which the Parliament of Canada might legislate for the preservation of peace, order and good government.

In the city of Montreal in the mid-1940s, large scale arrests were carried out by the police of young men and women whom they found going from door to door spreading their religion and distributing the periodicals "The Watchtower" and "Awake". These arrests were for breaches of a by-law requiring a licence for peddling any kind of wares. It is estimated that over 1,000 arrests were made. However, because the Jehovah's Witnesses disputed the charge, even though the fine was only $40.00, they were kept in jail until bail could be raised.

Frank Roncarelli was the owner of a well-known and highly respected restaurant in Montreal. He, and his father before him, had operated the restaurant, which was licensed for the sale of liquor, for approximately 34 years. Roncarelli, however, was also a Jehovah's Witness. Because he was a person of some means, he was accepted by the Recorder's Court as bail without any question. Indeed, up to November 12, 1946, he had gone security in about 380 cases, some of which included accused involved in repeated offences. His word was so respected that at times, to avoid delay when he was absent from the city, recognizances were signed by him in blank and kept ready for completion by the Court officials.

No sooner were members of the Jehovah's Witnesses arrested than they were released and back out on the streets pressing their religious beliefs on Montrealers. Roncarelli was obviously frustrating Premier Duplessis' scheme to rid the streets of Montreal of the Witnesses. Although Roncarelli, himself, was not taking part in the distribution of any material, he was obviously aiding others to do so.

As far as the authorities were concerned, his liquor licence was a "privilege" granted by the province. The profit which Roncarelli derived from the sale of liquor was being used to promote the disturbance of settled beliefs and generally arouse community dissatisfaction. Duplessis, who was the Attorney General as well as Prime Minister of Quebec, accepted the role of guardian and protector of these established beliefs. He believed that it was his duty and responsibility to punish Roncarelli and to warn others of what might happen if they persisted in similar activity on behalf of the Witnesses. On December 4, 1946, Duplessis cancelled Roncarelli's liquor licence. The effect was disastrous. He tried to operate his restaurant without a liquor licence for six months but found that it was no longer profitable. And so he closed it down and sold it.

However, Frank Roncarelli was not prepared to quietly leave the scene. On June 3, 1947, he sued Maurice Duplessis for the sum of $118,741.00. He argued that the Premier had cancelled the licence arbitrarily as an act of reprisal for his support of the Witnesses. Mr. Justice MacKinnon of the Quebec Superior Court agreed and awarded him damages of $8,123.53.

Duplessis appealed arguing that he had done nothing wrong because he honestly believed he was fulfilling his duty to the people of the province. Roncarelli cross-appealed arguing that the damages were too low. The case eventually reached the Supreme Court of Canada. There, in a majority decision of the Court, the judgment of the trial judge was sustained but it was increased by an additional $25,000.

To the argument that Duplessis, as Attorney General, was only acting to suppress or to prevent crimes and offences, Mr. Justice Martland had this to say:

> This amounts to a contention that he is free to use any methods he chooses; that, on suspicion of participation in what he thinks would be an offence, he may sentence a citizen to economic ruin without trial. This seems to me to be a very dangerous proposition and one which is completely alien to the legal concepts applicable to the administration of public office in Quebec, as well as in other Provinces of Canada.

On Sunday afternoon, September 4, 1949, three officers of the Quebec provincial police, dressed in their uniform, entered the yard of Esymier Chaput in the village of Chapeau, Quebec. Chaput, a Jehovah's Witness, was holding a religious meeting in his home. He had invited 30 people. Mr. Gotthold, a minister of that sect from Ottawa, had been invited to address the meeting.

When Chaput saw the officers outside of his home, he went out to see what they wanted. Constable Roger Chartrand, who was in charge of the investigation, asked if he and his two colleagues could enter. Chaput invited them in.

After watching the ceremony for a few minutes, Chartrand said that he was going to have to break up the meeting and everybody had to leave. Gotthold asked to be allowed to finish as he only had 20 minutes more to go but Chartrand refused and quickly grabbed the Bible out of his hand. The other officers then gathered up all of the other literature and Bibles in the room and took them out to their police cruiser.

In a few minutes, the officers returned. They told Gotthold that he would have to stop preaching. He asked if he was under arrest and Chartrand told him that he was not. When he said that he was not going to stop, another officer, Constable Young, proceeded to arrest Gotthold and placed him in the police cruiser. The other members of the congregation present were told to get out of Chaput's home and they quickly left.

Gotthold was then driven by the officers to the ferry which travels across the Ottawa River between Chapeau and Pembroke, Ontario, and was placed physically on the ferry. No charges of any kind were ever laid against anyone nor were any of the articles seized returned.

Esymier Chaput sued the three officers for damages. Chartrand defended his actions and those of his colleagues on the basis that they were charged with the duty "to keep law and order and prevent any trouble which might occur." When he was asked how he believed that his actions were "maintaining law and order" he said that, according to his information,

> There was a lot of people against that and that is why we were sent down there to maintain law and order in case there would be trouble . . . we were ordered to dismiss the meeting.

Chartrand had been led to believe that the activities of the Witnesses were illegal.

> Of course we understand that's illegal in Quebec, and that's the reason why there were no other questions necessary.
>
> Q. You understand it is illegal in Quebec?
>
> A. That's what I'm given to understand.
>
> Q. What gave you the impression it was illegal for Jehovah's Witnesses to hold meetings in Quebec?
>
> A. Well, I read it in the papers — I don't know — and their meetings were stopped.
>
> Q. Where?
>
> A. I read it in the paper; I don't know the place.
>
> Q. You never bothered about the law, to see if it was illegal?
>
> A. No; I have nothing to do with that.

In the Superior Court of Quebec, Chaput's claim for damages was dismissed. As far as the Court was concerned, the police officers were quite justified in their actions. Nine members of the Supreme Court of Canada, however, did not agree and reversed the judgment. Mr. Justice Taschereau called the conduct of the officers highly reprehensible:

> Je n'ai pas de doute que les trois intimés ont posé un acte hautement repréhensible, de nature à blesser profondemént la demandeur-appelant. En effet, il avait le droit indiscutable de convoquer dans sa demeure, l'assemblée où se sont réunies environ quarante personnes, et d'y convier Gotthold en sa qualité de prédicateur. Dans notre pays, il n'existe pas de religion d'Etat. Personne n'est tenu d'adhérer à une croyance quelconque. Toutes les religions sont sur un pied d'égalité, et tous les catholiques comme d'ailleurs tous les protestants, les juifs, ou les autres adhérents des diverses dénominations religieuses, ont la plus entière liberté de penser comme ils le désirent. La conscience de chacun est une affaire personelle, et l'affaire de nul autre. Il serait désolant de penser qu'une majorité puisse imposer ses vues religieuses à une minorité. Ce serait une erreur fâcheuse de croire qu'on sert son pays ou sa religion, en refusant dans une province, à une minorité, les mêmes droits que l'on revendique soi-même avec raison, dans une autre province.
>
> Mais dans les circonstances de la présente cause, on ne faisait qu'exposer des doctrines religieuses, sans doute contraires aux vues de la majorité des citoyens de la localité, mais l'opinion d'une minorité a droit au même respect que celle de la majorité.

> There is no doubt that the three respondents committed a highly reprehensible act which was deeply offensive to the appellant. He had the indisputable right to convene in his home a meeting of forty people and to ask Gotthold to speak in his capacity as minister. In our country, there does not exist a state religion. No one is required to follow someone else's belief. All religions are on the same footing and all catholics as well as others such as protestants, jews, or other adherents of different religious faiths have complete freedom to believe as they wish. The conscience of everyone is a personal affair and not that of anyone else. It would be terrible to think that a majority could impose their religious views on a minority. It would be deplorable if one could follow his own religion in his province and yet refuse to a minority in that province the same rights that he would quite properly claim in another province.
>
> In the circumstances of this present case, there were religious doctrines which were without doubt contrary to the views of a majority of citizens in that community, but the opinion of the minority has the same right of respect as that of the majority.

As the trial judge had dismissed the action and had not assessed the damages, he awarded Chaput $2,000 damages against the officers together with his court costs.

## Religious Freedom in America

There was probably no freedom as important as freedom of religion to those refugees who had escaped religious persecution in Great Britain and Europe to settle in the thirteen states which issued their famous Declaration of Independence on July 4, 1776. So important was this freedom that it was the first to be enshrined in the Amendments to the Constitution. But one of the ironies of life is that those who claim to have been religiously or politically persecuted, sometimes show little tolerance for the religious and political views of others. This was the case with the Puritans who had sought refuge in the New World from religious persecution in England. No sooner had they found themselves in control of a colonial government than they passed laws making their own religion the official religion of the colony. In time the persecuted became the persecutors.

It was for this reason that in the mid 1780s a group led by James Madison and Thomas Jefferson who, not members themselves of any minority religious group, nevertheless opposed all religious establishment. Their voice was successful in assuring that the First Amendment would include a non-establishment clause.

The First Amendment to the Constitution of the United States provides that,

> Congress shall make no laws respecting an establishment of religion, or prohibiting the free exercise thereof; . . .

In the 1930s, fascism was rising in Europe and America was experiencing its own brand of nationalistic fervour. Some school boards across the country adopted resolutions requiring students to salute the flag as part of their daily school ritual. Any child who refused to do so could be expelled and was then considered to be unlawfully absent and a delinquent. This meant that their parents or guardians could be prosecuted. Once more members of the Jehovah's Witnesses sect came into conflict with the law.

The Witnesses interpret the Bible literally. They believe that the flag is a "graven image" and that a requirement to salute it forces them to disobey God's command as revealed through the old testament book of Exodus, chapter 20, verses 3-5:

> 3. Thou shalt have no other gods before me.
> 4. Thou shalt not make unto thee any graven image, or any likeness of anything that is in heaven above, or that is in the earth beneath, or that is in the water under the earth.
> 5. Thou shalt not bow down thyself to them, nor serve them. . . .

The local school board in Minersville, Pennsylvania, a community with a population of less than 10,000 had passed a resolution requiring the pupils to salute the flag as part of the daily school routine. The children of Walter Gobitis, a Jehovah's Witness refused to comply. The youngest, Billy aged 10 wrote a letter on November 6, 1935 to his teacher explaining that it was contrary to his religious beliefs. Billy and his elder sister Lillian, age 12 were immediately expelled. Walter Gobitis hired a lawyer who successfully obtained an injunction from the District Court in Philadelphia restraining the school board from continuing to require the flag salute as a condition of the children's attendance in school. It was the Court's view that "no man, even though he be a school director or a judge, is empowered to censure another's religious convictions or set bounds to the areas of human conduct in which these convictions should be permitted to control his actions, unless compelled to do so by an overriding public necessity." That decision was upheld by the Court of Appeal.

Five years later, however, it was reversed by the Supreme Court of the United States with one lone dissenter. Mr. Justice Frankfurter, who delivered the judgment of the Court, believed that the role and duty of the courts was to exercise self restraint and not interfere with legislative enactments except as a last resort. He felt that the legislatures of the various states were entitled to preserve "the kind of ordered society which is summarized by our flag" through compulsory flag saluting. It was not the function of the Court to question the "wisdom of training children in patriotic impulses by these compulsions" even though the members of the Court were convinced of the "folly of such a measure."

Mr. Justice Harlan Fiske Stone, who was later to become Chief Justice of the Court, delivered an eloquent dissent:

> History teaches us that there have been but few infringements of personal liberty by the state which have not been justified, as they are here, in the name of righteousness and public good, and few which have not been directed, as they are now, at politically helpless minorities. The framers were not unaware that under the system which they created most governmental curtailments of personal liberty would have the support of a legislative judgment that the public interest would be better served by its curtailment than by its constitutional protection. I cannot conceive that in prescribing, as limitations upon the powers of government, the freedom of the mind and spirit secured by the explicit guaranties of freedom of speech and religion, they intended or rightly could have left any latitude for a legislative judgment that the compulsory expression of belief which violates religious convictions would better serve the public interest than their protection. The Constitution may well elicit expressions of loyalty to it and to the government which it created, but it does not command such expressions or otherwise give any indication that compulsory expressions of loyalty play any such part in our scheme of government as to override the constitutional protection of freedom of speech and religion. And while such expressions of loyalty, when voluntarily given, may promote national unity, it is quite another matter to say that their compulsory expression by children in violation of their own and their parents' religious convictions can be regarded as playing so important a part in our national unity as to leave school boards free to exact it despite the constitutional guaranty of freedom of religion.

The Gobitis decision was delivered on June 3, 1940, a time when patriotic fervour had reached its peak in America. Europe was almost under the control of Hitler's seemingly invincible forces. In America, in various parts of the country, the Witnesses came under attack by angry mobs who burned down religious meeting halls, broke up meetings and even in some cases, had members removed from their community. Flag salute, which had been intended to symbolize the American notion of freedom, now became an instrument of oppression of a religious minority.

This had the opposite effect upon commentators everywhere who pointed to the Gobitis decision as the reason for the violence. Others, such as the West Virginia legislature found the impetus in the decision to amend their own laws to require all the schools in the state to teach, foster and perpetuate the "ideals, principles and spirit of Americanism." All teachers and pupils were required to salute the flag and their refusal was considered an act of insubordination which subjected them to expulsion and possible prosecution for delinquency. When a number of Witnesses' children were expelled from public schools in West Virginia for refusal to salute the flag, Walter Barnette applied for an injunction to restrain the school boards from enforcing the statute. Again the District Court granted the injunction and it eventually was heard by the Supreme Court of the United States.

This time, the composition of the Court had changed. Three judges of the Court, Justices Black, Douglas and Murphy refuted their earlier support of the majority in the Gobitis case. Mr. Justice Stone was now Chief Justice and another eloquent liberal, Robert H. Jackson had been appointed to the Court. Mr. Justice Jackson delivered a judgment upholding the injunction and declaring the West Virginia statute unconstitutional. He accepted the argument that censorship or suppression of expression of opinion was tolerated by the Constitution when the expression presented "a clear and present danger of action of a kind that the State was empowered to prevent and punish." However, he rejected the notion espoused by Mr. Justice Frankfurter that the courts should not interfere with state legislatures who sought to promote national unity through the flag salute:

> The very purpose of a Bill of Rights was to withdraw certain subjects from the vicissitudes of political controversy, to place them beyond the reach of majorities and officials and to establish them as legal principles to be applied by the Courts. One's right to life, liberty, and property, to free speech, a free press, freedom of worship and assembly, and other fundamental rights may not be submitted to vote; they depend on the outcome of no elections.

He went on,

> Struggles to coerce uniformity of sentiment in support of some end thought essential to their time and country have been waged by many good as well as by evil men. Nationalism is a relatively recent phenomenon, but at other times and places the ends have been racial or territorial security, support of a dynasty or regime, and particular plans for saving souls. As first and moderate methods to attain unity have failed, those bent on its accomplishment must resort to an ever-increasing severity.

> Ultimate futility of such attempts to compel coherence is the lesson of every such effort from the Roman drive to stamp out Christianity as a disturber of its pagan unity, the Inquisition, as a means to religious and dynastic unity, the Siberian exiles as means to Russian unity, down to the fast failing efforts of our present totalitarian enemies. Those who begin coercive elimination of dissent soon find themselves exterminating dissenters. Compulsory unification of opinion achieves only the unanimity of the graveyard.

And finally,

> But freedom to differ is not limited to things that do not matter much. That would be a mere shadow of freedom. The test of its substance is the right to differ as to things that touch the heart of the existing order.

Until recently, the "establishment of religion" clause has provoked little controversy. However, after the Second World War, two forms of religious instruction in the school did bring into question the meaning of that expression. The first, popularly called the "released time" cases, referred to a programme under which clergymen of various faiths — protestant, catholic and jewish — gave religious instruction to public school children during school hours. Students who agreed to take religious instruction were released to attend those classes. Students who did not wish to take religious instruction could not leave the school; they had to leave their classroom for another room in the school to participate in some other non-religious activity. The second controversy centred around the requirement of prayers in public schools.

In 1948, the Supreme Court of the United States, in *McCollum v. Board of Education* found the "released time" programme unconstitutional because it used tax-supported property for religious instruction in violation of the establishment clause of the First Amendment. Mr. Justice Black, who delivered the Court's judgment, considered that the purpose of the First Amendment was to separate church and state. He believed this was not being accomplished where the state was helping to provide pupils for their religious classes "through the use of the state's compulsory public school machinery."

Americans on the threshold of a religious revival spurred on by the advent of the nuclear age were bitterly critical of the decision. Their criticism encouraged New York City to create its own released-time programme. The difference between this one, and that of Illinois which had spawned the McCollum case, was that in New York City, the students were released to take religious instruction in buildings outside the school boundaries. This time an attack on the programme was not successful. In *Zorach v. Clauson*, the Supreme Court, with the criticism of the McCollum case still ringing in their ears, upheld the programme because tax-supported public school buildings were not being used.

Justices Black and Jackson dissented. Mr. Justice Black noted that,

> The state thus makes religious sects beneficiaries of its power to compel children to attend secular schools. Any use of such coercive power by the state to help or hinder some religious sects or to prefer all religious sects over non-believers or vice versa is just what I think the First Amendment forbids. In considering whether the state has entered this forbidden field the question is not whether it has entered too far but whether it has entered at all. New York is manipulating its compulsory education laws to help religious sects get pupils. This is not separation but combination of Church and State.

And Mr. Justice Jackson felt that the programme,

serves as a temporary jail for a pupil who will not go to Church. It takes more subtlety of mind than I possess to deny that this is governmental constraint in support of religion. It is as unconstitutional, in my view, when exerted by indirection as when exercised forthrightly.

A more contentious issue, however, was the use of prayers in public schools. In November 1951, the New York State Board of Regents, which supervises the state's public school system, recommended that local school boards adopt a non-sectarian prayer to be recited by the students. In 1958, the New Hyde Park Public School Board adopted that recommendation and directed the principal to cause the prayer to be said aloud by each class in the presence of a teacher at the beginning of each school day. Lawrence Roth and Steven Engel who each had two children in the school were offended with the direction. After organizing a number of parents, they applied for an order by way of *mandamus* to compel the board to discontinue the use of the prayer. Both the trial court and the New York Court of Appeal refused the application finding that the guarantee of freedom of religion had not been infringed because the daily recitation of the prayer was not compulsory. Four years later on April 3, 1962, *Engel v. Vitale et al.* was heard by the Supreme Court of the United States. The Court, with a lone dissenter, found the programme unconstitutional because it infringed the establishment clause.

Mr. Justice Black who delivered the opinion of the Court observed:

> When the power, prestige and financial support of government is placed behind a particular religious belief, the indirect coercive pressure upon religious minorities to conform to the prevailing officially approved religion is plain. But the purposes underlying the Establishment Clause go much further than that. Its first and most immediate purpose rested on the belief that a union of government and religion tends to destroy government and to degrade religion. The history of governmentally established religion, both in England and in this country, showed that whenever government had allied itself with one particular form of religion, the inevitable result had been that it had incurred the hatred, disrespect and even contempt of those who held contrary beliefs. That same history showed that many people had lost their respect for any religion that had relied upon the support of government to spread its faith. The Establishment Clause thus stands as an expression of principle on the part of the Founders of our Constitution that religion is too personal, too sacred, too holy, to permit its "unhallowed perversion" by a civil magistrate.

To those who argued that this interpretation of the Constitution would only show the Court's hostility towards religion or prayer, he had this reply:

> These men [the founding fathers] knew that the First Amendment, which tried to put an end to governmental control of religion and of prayer, was not written to destroy either. They knew rather that it was written to quiet well-justified fears which nearly all of them felt arising out of an awareness that governments of the past had shackled men's tongues to make them speak only the religious thoughts that government wanted them to speak and to pray only to the God that government wanted them to pray to. It is neither

sacrilegious nor antireligious to say that each separate government in this country should stay out of the business of writing or sanctioning official prayers and leave that purely religious function to the people themselves and to those the people choose to look to for religious guidance.

The decision understandably aroused a storm of protest across the country. Cardinal Spellmen attacked it because it struck "at the very heart of the Godly tradition in which America's children have for so long been raised." Billy Graham complained that he thought that the Constitution meant that "we were to have freedom of religion, not freedom from religion." There were even proposals in Congress to nullify the decision by constitutional amendment. It was in this atmosphere and under this pressure that in the following year the Supreme Court was faced with two more cases involving Bible reading and the recitation of the Lord's Prayer in public schools. The Court, however, stood firm in its determination to withstand the criticism.

The first case, *Abbington School District v. Schempp*, concerned a Pennsylvania state law which required at least 10 verses from the Bible to be read at the beginning of each school day. Any child could be excused from attendance with the written consent of his parent or guardian. The second, *Murray v. Curlett* related to a rule passed by the Baltimore Board of School Commissioners which required either the reading of a chapter in the Bible or the use of the Lord's Prayer for the opening of public school exercises. Both were found to be unconstitutional by a unanimous Supreme Court. Mr. Justice Clark summed up the Court's view:

The place of religion in our society is an exalted one, achieved through a long tradition of reliance on the home, the church and inviolable citadel of the human heart and mind. We have come to recognize through bitter experience that it is not within the power of government to invade that citadel, whether its purpose or effect be to aid or oppose, to advance or retard. In the relationship between man and religion, the State is firmly committed to a position of neutrality. Though the application of that rule requires interpretation of a delicate sort, the rule itself is clearly and concisely stated in the words of the First Amendment.

## Freedom of Religion Under the Canadian Charter

The Charter of Rights and Freedoms, 1982 extended the guarantee of "freedom of religion" contained in the Bill of Rights to "freedom of conscience and religion". But it did not go so far as to ensure against "an establishment of religion" as the First Amendment. This may have been deliberate when we notice that the preamble to the Charter provides that Canada "is founded upon principles that recognize the supremacy of God and the rule of law...." Nevertheless, "freedom of conscience" was undoubtedly intended to encompass something more than simply "freedom of religion." It was intended to protect those who have no religion at all and to respect their right not to be even subtly coerced to embrace any religion. It is not surprising, therefore, that the first statute to come under attack was the Lord's Day Act which the Supreme Court of Canada had decided, 20 years earlier, did not offend the freedom of religion clause in the Bill of Rights.

Section 4 of the Lord's Day Act makes it an offence to sell or purchase any goods or real estate, or to carry on any business on Sunday. Although this federal statute only came into force in Canada on March 1, 1907, it has a much longer history in English law. The observance of the Christian Sabbath, under threat of secular sanction, can be traced back as early as Saxon times. The first major statute, the Sunday Fairs Act, was passed in England in 1448 prohibiting all fairs and markets on Sunday. Over succeeding centuries, a number of other statutes were enacted to prohibit all sorts of activity on Sunday. The purpose of the laws was to encourage public and private piety. With the adoption of English law these statutes came into force in Canada in 1762. Thereafter, the provinces, such as Ontario, took up the cause of religious piety and passed laws from time to time restricting activities on Sunday. Such legislation continued even after Confederation in 1867. However, it stopped in 1903 when the Judicial Committee of the Privy Council decided in *Attorney General of Ontario v. Hamilton Street Railway* that the Ontario statute known as "An Act to prevent the profanation of the Lord's Day" went beyond provincial powers because it intruded into the federal field of criminal law. It was then that the Parliament of Canada stepped in and passed the Lord's Day Act in 1907.

The first challenge to the Lord's Day Act, on the grounds that it infringed "freedom of religion" guaranteed by the Bill of Rights, came shortly after the Bill was passed in 1960. In *Robertson and Rosetanni v. The Queen*, the Supreme Court of Canada found this "legislation for the preservation of the sanctity of Sunday" did not affect "freedom of religion". Mr. Justice Ritchie who delivered the judgment of the majority felt that,

> The practical result of this law on those whose religion requires them to observe a day of rest other than Sunday, is a purely secular and financial one in that they are required to refrain from carrying on or conducting their business on Sunday as well as on their day of rest. In some cases this is no doubt a business inconvenience, but it is neither an abrogation nor an abridgment nor an infringement of religious freedom, and the fact that it has been brought about by reason of the existence of a statute enacted for the purpose of preserving the sanctity of Sunday, cannot, in my view, be construed as attaching some religious significance to an effect which is purely secular in so far as non-Christians are concerned.

But Mr. Justice Cartwright, who was later to become Chief Justice, strongly disagreed. As far as he was concerned,

> . . . a law which compels a course of conduct, whether positive or negative, for a purely religious purpose infringes the freedom of religion.

> A law, which, on solely religious grounds, forbids the pursuit on Sunday of an otherwise lawful activity differs in degree, perhaps, but not in kind from a law which commands a purely religious course of conduct on that day, such as for example, the attendance at least once at divine service in a specified church.

It is significant that in the same year, an opposite conclusion was reached by the Supreme Court of the United States in *Sherbert v. Verner*. In that case a woman lost her job because she refused to work on Sunday and was denied benefits under state unemployment legislation on the ground that she was "not available" to work. Mr. Justice Brennan, delivering the judgment of the Court, felt that the denial affected the "free exercise" of her religion:

> The ruling forces her to choose between following the precepts of her religion and for-feiting benefits, on the one hand, and abandoning one of the precepts of her religion in order to accept work, on the other hand. Governmental imposition of such a choice puts the same kind of burden upon the free exercise of religion as would a fine imposed against appellant for her Saturday worship.

Shortly after the Charter of Rights and Freedoms came into existence, the Lord's Day Act was again tested. On Sunday, May 30, 1982, officers of the Calgary City Police went to the Big M Drug Mart Store and watched clerks selling groceries, plastic cups and a bicycle padlock. The police charged the store with a breach of section 4 of the Lord's Day Act but the case was dismissed by a Provincial Court Judge because he considered that the Act breached freedom of conscience and religion guaranteed by the Charter. A split panel of the Alberta Court of Appeal agreed. Mr. Justice Laycraft speaking for the majority felt that the Court was not bound by the previous decision of the Supreme Court of Canada:

> The most fundamental difference between the Charter and the Bill is the enhanced status of the Charter as part of the "supreme law of Canada" (s. 52(1) of the *Constitution Act, 1982*). It is not merely a declaration of existing law or a tool for use in statutory construction. By s. 24 the judiciary is charged with the task of devising appropriate remedies for infringement. This enhanced status of the Charter, as well as the different language in it, requires the conclusion, in my opinion, that *Robertson and Rosetanni* does not apply to Charter cases. It does not preclude a finding by this court that the *Lord's Day Act* infringes the fundamental freedom of religion and conscience given by the Charter.

As far as he was concerned, he could not see the Act as merely a "business inconvenience".

> [E]mphasis on economic effects alone ignores an even more serious burden: the coercive effect of the statute in imposing the Christian Sunday on all persons, Christians and non-Christians, alike. Good citizens obey the law; for many Canadians able to bear or ignore any economic penalty of obedience, the imposition of the Christian Sunday using the force of the State to do it far outweighs any economic consideration.
>    ... the moral power of the State has been imposed on one side of a dispute between its citizens in which the State must take no part. Thereby, there has occurred a serious infringement of the fundamental freedom of conscience and religion.

Mr. Justice Belzil, in dissent, was concerned that such an interpretation would strip away all vestiges of values and traditions which we have inherited:

> Such interpretation would make of the Charter an instrument for the repression of the majority at the instance of every dissident and result in an amorphous, rootless and godless nation contrary to the recognition of the Supremacy of God declared in the preamble.

On April 24, 1985, the Supreme Court of Canada unanimously upheld the decision of the Alberta Court of Appeal. Chief Justice Dickson agreed that the purpose of the Lord's Day Act was the compulsion of religious observance.

> A truly free society is one which can accommodate a wide variety of beliefs, diversity of tastes and pursuits, customs and codes of conduct. A free society is one which aims at equality with respect to the enjoyment of fundamental freedoms and I say this without any reliance upon s. 15 of the Charter. Freedom must surely be founded in respect for the inherent dignity and the inviolable rights of the human person. The essence of the concept of freedom of religion is the right to entertain such religious beliefs as a person chooses, the right to declare religious beliefs openly and without fear of hindrance or reprisal, and the right to manifest religious belief by worship and practice or by teaching and dissemination. But the concept means more than that.

> Freedom can primarily be characterized by the absence of coercion or constraint. If a person is compelled by the State or the will of another to a course of action or inaction which he would not otherwise have chosen, he is not acting of his own volition and he cannot be said to be truly free. One of the major purposes of the Charter is to protect, within reason, from compulsion or restraint. Coercion includes not only such blatant forms of compulsion as direct commands to act or refrain from acting on pain of sanction, coercion includes indirect forms of control which determine or limit alternative courses of conduct available to others. Freedom in a broad sense embraces both the absence of coercion and constraint, and the right to manifest beliefs and practices. Freedom means that, subject to such limitations as are necessary to protect public safety, order, health, or morals or the fundamental rights and freedoms of others, no one is to be forced to act in a way contrary to his beliefs or his conscience.

> What may appear good and true to a majoritarian religious group, or to the State acting at their behest, may not, for religious reasons, be imposed upon citizens who take a contrary view. The Charter safeguards religious minorities from the threat of "the tyranny of the majority".

As far as he was concerned, the Lord's Day Act,

> [W]orks a form of coercion inimical to the spirit of the Charter and the dignity of all non-Christians. In proclaiming the standards of the Christian faith, the Act creates a climate hostile to, and gives the appearance of discrimination against, non-Christian Canadians. It takes religious values rooted in Christian morality and, using the force of the State, translates them into a positive law binding on believers and non-believers alike. The theological content of the legislation remains as a subtle and constant reminder to religious minorities within the country of their differences with, and alienation from, the dominant religious culture.

He felt it necessary to stress, however, that,

[N]othing in these reasons should be read as suggesting any opposition to Sunday being spent as a religious day; quite the contrary. It is recognized that for a great number of Canadians, Sunday is the day when their souls rest in God, when the spiritual takes priority over the material, a day which, to them, gives security and meaning because it is linked to creation and the Creator. It is a day which brings a balanced perspective to life, an opportunity for man to be in communion with man and with God. In my view, however, as I read the Charter, it mandates that the legislative preservation of a Sunday day of rest should be secular, the diversity of belief and non-belief, the diverse socio-cultural backgrounds of Canadians make it constitutionally incompetent for the federal Parliament to provide legislative preference for any one religion at the expense of those of another religious persuasion.

But the guarantee of freedom of conscience and religion in the Charter did not mean that government had no power to compel a uniform day of rest from labour; it could do so provided that the law did not compel observance of Sunday by virtue of its religious significance. If a statute could be passed specifying a particular day as a day of rest, so long as it did not have religious significance, then only the provinces could enact such legislation under its exclusive power to deal with "property and civil rights in the province".

In 1975, the Ontario Legislature passed the Retail Business Holidays Act. Section 2 of the Act prohibits the carrying on of certain retail business activity on holidays as defined in the Act, including Sunday. No sooner was the Charter passed than a number of retail businesses decided to challenge the law as infringing their right to freedom of conscience or religion. One of the businesses, Nortown Foods Ltd., was owned by Orthodox Jews whose religion required them to be closed on Saturday. The others were owned by persons who did not observe any day other than Sunday as a religious holiday. On September 19, 1984 the Ontario Court of Appeal in *Regina v. Videoflicks Ltd.* upheld the conviction of everyone except Nortown Foods Ltd.

Mr. Justice Tarnopolsky in delivering the judgment of the Court, accepted the argument that freedom of religion goes beyond the ability to hold certain beliefs without coercion and restraint and entails more than the ability to profess those beliefs openly. As far as he was concerned, freedom of religion also includes the right to "observe the essential practices demanded by the tenets of one's religion". In determining what those practices are in any given case, the analysis had to proceed not from the majority's perspective of the concept of religion but "in terms of the role that the practices and beliefs assume in the religion of the individual or group concerned." However, freedom of conscience was not the mere decision of any individual on any particular occasion to act or not act in a certain way. For the right to be protected constitutionally,

[T]he behaviour or practice in question would have to be based upon a set of beliefs by which one feels bound to conduct most, if not all, of one's voluntary actions. While freedom of conscience necessarily includes the right not to have a religious basis for one's conduct, it does not follow that one can rely upon the Charter protection of freedom of conscience to object to an enforced holiday simply because it happens to coincide with someone else's sabbath. Rather, to make such an objection one would have to demonstrate, based upon genuine beliefs and regular observance, that one holds as a sacrosanct day of rest a day other than Sunday and is thereby forced to close one's business on that day as well as on the enforced holiday.

He considered that the Act was not concerned with compelling observance of the sabbath of the majority Christian religion nor was its effect to impose that view upon society at large. However, the owners of Nortown Foods Ltd. were affected dramatically because they sincerely observed a day other than Sunday as a sabbath and thus had to close their business establishment two days. Since the Act prohibited certain practices of the owners of Nortown Foods Ltd., which were an essential part of their religion, even though the impact on religion occurred in an indirect sense, it infringed their freedom of religion and was of no force and effect insofar as it concerned them.

# 3

# Freedom of Thought, Belief, Opinion and Expression

If all mankind minus one were of one opinion, and only one person were of the contrary opinion, mankind would be no more justified in silencing that one person, than he, if he had the power, would be justified in silencing mankind. Were an opinion a personal possession of no value except to the owner; if to be obstructed in the enjoyment of it were simply a private injury, it would make some difference whether the injury was inflicted only on a few persons or on many. But the peculiar evil of silencing the expression of an opinion is, that it is robbing the human race; posterity as well as the existing generation; those who dissent from the opinion, still more than those who hold it. If the opinion is right, they are deprived of the opportunity of exchanging error for truth: if wrong, they lose, what is almost as great a benefit, the clearer perception and livelier impression of truth, produced by its collision with error.

John Stuart Mill, On Liberty (1859)

The vitality of civil and political institutions in our society depends on free discussion. . . It is only through free debate and free exchange of ideas that government remains responsible to the will of the people and peaceful change is effected. The right to speak freely and to promote diversity of ideas and programmes is therefore one of the chief distinctions that sets us apart from totalitarian regimes.

Accordingly a function of free speech under our system of government is to invite dispute. It may indeed best serve its high purpose when it induces a condition of unrest, creates dissatisfaction with conditions as they are, or even stirs people to anger. Speech is often provocative and challenging. It may strike at prejudices and pre-conceptions and have profound unsettling effects as it presses for acceptance of an idea. That is why freedom of speech, though not absolute, . . . is nevertheless protected against censorship or punishment, unless shown likely to produce a clear and present danger of a serious substantive evil that rises far above public inconvenience, annoyance or unrest. . . There is no room under our Constitution for a more restrictive view. For the alternative would lead to standardization of ideas either by legislatures, courts, or dominant political or community groups.

Mr. Justice William O. Douglas, *Terminiello v. Chicago* (1949)

On December 27, 1839, the H.M.S. Beagle, under the command of Captain Robert Fitzroy, started out on a five-year voyage around the world. It was a scientific mission — to survey the seas for the British Admiralty. On board was a 22-year-old recently-graduated English divinity student, Charles Darwin, who had signed on for the voyage as an unpaid naturalist. At that point of his life, Darwin had never questioned his religious beliefs. In his words, "I did not then in the least doubt the strict and literal truth of every word in the Bible." What Darwin saw during that voyage was to sow the seeds of doubt that would change his entire life and that of mankind. In 1859, he published the conclusions he reached from that voyage in a book, *The Origin of Species.*

For 2,000 years people of the Christian world had been taught that God had constructed the world in six days, and had made the first man in his own image and called him Adam. Those who had dared to question these beliefs had been arrested and burned at the stake for their doubts. The famous Italian astronomer, Galileo, who dared to suggest that the earth revolved around the sun and was not the centre of the universe, was arrested by the Inquisition in Rome in 1633. He was ordered to recant and forced to spend the last eight years of his life under house arrest.

Darwin now suggested that the world was not 6,000 years old as was believed in orthodox Christian circles but was millions of years old. Over the years man himself had evolved from a simpler form of life, probably from the single-celled protozoa. Man had survived and developed at the top of the animal species because he was able to adapt better to his environment than any other animal. This Darwin called "natural selection."

Although the idea of evolution had been conceived long before Darwin, no one up to that time had collected and analyzed the evidence the way he had. Understandably, *The Origin of Species* created a storm of controversy in England, culminating in 1860, at the British Association meeting at Oxford, in the famous debate between T.H. Huxley and Bishop Samuel Wilberforce.

In the United States, the theory of evolution was quickly embraced by the scientific community who taught in the so-called "liberal" universities of the northeast, and was introduced to their students. Even theologians began to accept that the theory was not against the teachings of the church. However, the rural south and western parts of the United States, which had been nurtured on the preachings of fundamental evangelists, believed that the theory of evolution would only unloose "adultery, drunkenness and social dishonour."

The paladin of fundamentalist views was William Jennings Bryan who had been defeated three times for the presidency of the United States. Defending the case of free thinking was Clarence Darrow, an avowed agnostic who was probably the most famous criminal lawyer in the country. In the summer of 1925, in the little town of Dayton, Tennessee, these two champions of opposing views clashed on a battlefield. In 1925 the state of Tennessee had passed a statute known as the Butler Act which prohibited the teaching of evolutionary theory in all Tennessee schools. John Scopes, a 24-year-old science teacher and coach of the high school football team, had mentioned to some friends that he had been teaching the Darwinian theory to his students. They decided to test the law and Scopes agreed to make the necessary admission and stand trial.

The trial began on July 10, 1925. While all of America watched, newspaper reporters from across the United States crowded into Dayton to report the daily proceedings. William Jennings Bryan, who was then 65 years old, was retained as a member of the prosecution team. Clarence Darrow, three years older, was hired by the American Civil Liberties Union to be one of the defence counsel. The sole issue was whether Scopes had taught evolution contrary to the Butler Act. But Darrow and the other counsel for the defence wanted the opportunity to demonstrate that a strict and literal interpretation of the Bible would only lead to absurdity. They asked for the opportunity to call a number of expert witnesses, not only scientists but also theologians, to give evidence about the theory of evolution. The trial judge, Judge Raulston denied the request. The defence decided to try a different tactic. They asked permission to call William Jennings Bryan to give evidence for the defence. Bryan had the right to refuse to do so and Judge Raulston would have supported him. But Bryan, confident that he would now find a forum for his views, agreed to testify. His decision to do so turned out to be foolhardy. Darrow now had the upper hand and the questions he put to Bryan completely destroyed Bryan's credibility. Some of the questions and answers went like this:

DARROW: Do you claim that everything in the Bible should be literally interpreted?
BRYAN: I believe everything in the Bible should be accepted as it is given there.

Darrow then wanted to know about the book of Joshua and whether Joshua had made the sun stand still or the earth stand still. Bryan conceded that it might have been the earth.

DARROW: Have you ever pondered what would have happened to the earth if it had stood still?
BRYAN: No.
DARROW: You have not?
BRYAN: No; the God I believe in could have taken care of that, Mr. Darrow.
DARROW: I see. Have you ever pondered what would naturally happen to the earth if it stood still suddenly?
BRYAN: No.
DARROW: You know it would have been converted into a molten mass of matter?

Bryan did not answer.

Darrow then asked Bryan when the Flood took place. Bryan answered that he did not know.

DARROW: What do you think?
BRYAN: I do not think about things I don't think about.
DARROW: Do you think about things you do think about?
BRYAN: Well, sometimes.

Darrow then read from the Bible:

And the Lord God said unto the serpent, Because thou hast done this thou art cursed above all cattle and above every beast of the field; upon thy belly shalt thou go and dust shalt thou eat all the days of thy life.

He then asked Bryan,

Do you think that this is why the serpent is compelled to crawl upon its belly?
BRYAN: I believe that.
DARROW: Have you any idea how the snake went before that time?
BRYAN: No sir.
DARROW: Do you know whether he walked on his tail or not?
BRYAN: No, sir, I have no way to know.

Although Judge Raulston eventually ordered all of Bryan's evidence removed from the record and Scopes was convicted and fined $100, Darrow had achieved his purpose. He had clearly demonstrated what happens to even great men when they close their minds to the views of someone else.

But the battle was not over. Two more anti-evolution laws were passed, the first in Mississippi in 1925, the second in Arkansas in 1927. And, it was not until 1968 that the "anti-monkey" laws were finally struck down by the Supreme Court of the United States who held that the laws were unconstitutional because they established a religious doctrine violating both the First and Fourth Amendments to the Constitution.

What happened to John Scopes? He appealed his conviction to the Tennessee Supreme Court where it was overturned. The decision was not reversed because the Butler Act was unconstitutional as his lawyers had argued, but because there was some doubt as to his guilt. A new trial was ordered by the Court but it never took place. In the meantime, Scopes had left the state and it was decided to abandon the prosecution.

## The Struggle in England

Freedom of expression is the life blood of a democratic society. It is only with the free exchange of ideas to enlighten public opinion that a democratic society can survive and grow. Freedom of expression is occasionally the subject of abuse, as is illustrated by the words of Chief Justice Duff of the Supreme Court of Canada, in the *Alberta Press* case,

Even within its legal limits, it is liable to abuse and grave abuse, and such abuse is constantly exemplified before our eyes; but it is axiomatic that the practice of this right of free public discussion of public affairs, notwithstanding its incidental mischiefs, is the breath of life for parliamentary institutions.

To early English monarchs, freedom of expression was an anathema, a mischief that could not be tolerated if the Crown was to exercise absolute sovereignty. Any form of censure, whether justified or not, was forbidden in case the authority of the Crown would be diminished by it.

Tudor Kings and Queens were particularly sensitive to criticism. The Court of Star Chamber, created by Henry VII in 1487, was given authority to suppress any form of criticism of the Crown.

A few years earlier the printing press had been introduced into England and had become an effective method of spreading dissension. Henry and his successors were not prepared to tolerate any discussion which was hostile to the government. Consequently, it was during this period that the law of treason and seditious libel was developed and expanded by statute and by judges loyal to the Crown. Even members of Parliament could be prosecuted for any criticism of the Crown. The Speaker of the House, however, had the temerity to claim privilege of freedom of speech at the beginning of the 16th century. Sir Thomas Moore, the speaker in 1523, became more bold and asked for this privilege for all members. But as late as 1593, Queen Elizabeth, in granting the privilege, warned the members:

> Privilege of Speech is granted, but you must know what privilege you have; not to speak everyone what he listeth or what cometh in his brain to utter that; but your privilege is Aye or No.

The struggle for freedom of speech in the House of Commons continued during the reign of the Stuart Kings. Charles I ordered the prosecution and imprisonment of a few members who attacked him and directed that they not be released until they gave surety of good behaviour. But in 1649, Charles lost his head and the members he had imprisoned were released. Conflicts between the members of the House of Commons and Charles' successors continued even after the Restoration. The struggle was finally resolved during the reign of William and Mary. In 1689, the year of their coronation, the Bill of Rights was enacted. It provided that "freedome of speech, and debates of proceedings in Parlyament, ought not to be impeached or questioned in any court or place out of Parlyament."

## Freedom of Expression in the Thirteen Colonies

The American colonists regarded the right to criticize government so important that not only was freedom of speech guaranteed in the First Amendment but "the right of the people peaceably to assemble, and to petition the government for a redress of grievances" was also enshrined therein. However, no sooner was the first government in power than, in 1798, the Alien and Sedition Acts were passed by Congress. Their purpose was to prohibit any criticism of the Government of the United States including Congress, the Senate or the President, which would "bring them into contempt or disrepute or (to) excite against them the hatred of the good people of the United States." It was believed that unless such laws were passed, the newly established government institutions might be in jeopardy. Between 1798 and 1801 a number of people were successfully prosecuted. But, when Thomas Jefferson was elected President in 1801, he pardoned those convicted and the Sedition Act was eventually allowed to expire. Nevertheless, it was recognized that the states were allowed to prosecute anyone guilty of sedition. This view continued for another century.

The real test for freedom of speech began with the events of the First World War. In 1918, Congress passed the Espionage Act. According to this Act, when the United States was at war it became an offence to wilfully "make or convey false reports or false statements with the intent to interfere with the operation or success of the military or naval forces of the United States or to promote the success of its enemies"; to "wilfully cause or attempt to cause insubordination, disloyalty, mutiny, or refusal of duty, in the military or naval forces of the United States;" or to "wilfully obstruct the recruiting or enlistment service of the United States, to the injury of the United States."

The first and most important of the espionage cases to reach the Supreme Court of the United States was *Schenk v. United States.* Charles T. Schenk was the general secretary of the Socialist Party. In 1917, while American troops were fighting in France, he printed and distributed 15,000 leaflets to draftees urging them to oppose and resist the draft. He was charged with a breach of the Espionage Act and his conviction was upheld by the Supreme Court of the United States. Mr. Justice Holmes, delivering the unanimous judgment of the Court, formulated what was to be later known as his classic "clear and present danger" test. He expressed that opinion in these words:

> We admit that in many places and in ordinary times the defendants in saying all that was said in this circular would have been within their constitutional rights. The character of every act depends upon the circumstances in which it is done. The most stringent protection of free speech would not protect a man in falsely shouting fire in a theatre and causing a panic. It does not even protect a man from an injunction against uttering words that may have all the effect of force. The question in every case is whether the words are used in such circumstances and are of such a nature as to create a clear and present danger that they will bring about the substantive evils that Congress has a right to prevent. It is a question of proximity and degree. When a nation is at war many things that might be said in time of peace are such a hindrance to its effort that their utterance will not be endured so long as men fight and that no Court could regard them as protected by any constitutional right.

The United States was not at war in 1934 when Dirk DeJonge, along with three of his associates, was arrested by the Portland, Oregon police for violating the Oregon Criminal Syndicalism Act.

The Act made it an offence to advocate or teach by word of mouth or writing the use of physical violence, arson, destruction of property, sabotage, or other unlawful acts or methods as a means of accomplishing or effecting industrial or political ends, or as a means of effecting industrial or political revolution or for profit.

The Oregon Criminal Syndicalism Act was also designed to outlaw communism without actively saying so. DeJonge and his associates were dues paying members of the communist party. They believed that the constitutional guarantee of free speech and peaceable assembly entitled them to hold meetings to spread the ideas of their party.

On May 9, 1934, the International Longshoremen's Association called a general strike in Portland to protest that ship owners were not prepared to recognize their union as the bargaining agent for longshoremen. DeJonge and the local Communist Party decided to support the longshoremen and called a meeting for Friday evening, July 27, 1934. Approximately 150 to 300 people attended the meeting and a number of speeches were given, including one by DeJonge. None of the speakers advocated violence. Nevertheless, the Portland police arrived and arrested DeJonge and three other speakers and charged them with violating the Oregon Criminal Syndicalism Act.

At his trial, his lawyers argued that not only had no violence been advocated at the meeting, but that the statute violated DeJonge's right to assemble peaceably and his right to freedom of speech. These objections were dismissed and DeJonge was convicted and sentenced to seven years in prison.

His conviction, however, was reversed by the Supreme Court of the United States. As far as the Court was concerned, a state had no right to prevent any meetings whose object or purpose was peaceful political action. Chief Justice Hughes delivered the unanimous opinion of the Court in these words:

> The greater the importance of safeguarding the community from incitements to the overthrow of our institutions by force and violence, the more imperative is the need to preserve inviolate the constitutional rights of free speech, free press and free assembly in order to maintain the opportunity for free political discussion, to the end that government may be responsive to the will of the people and that changes, if desired, may be obtained by peaceful means. Therein lies the security of the Republic, the very foundation of constitutional government. ... The question, if the rights of free speech and peaceable assembly are to be preserved, is not as to the auspices under which the meeting is held but as to its purpose; not as to the relations of the speakers, but whether their utterances transcend the bounds of the freedom of speech which the Constitution protects.

Are there any limits on the right of free speech? History has shown us that the suppression of ideas is dangerous to the development of mankind. Democratic countries have always recognized that their survival is dependent upon the free exchange of ideas. Mr. Justice Holmes had argued that "the best test of truth is the power of the thought to get itself accepted in the competition of the market." His colleague, Mr. Justice Brandeis, who concurred in many of his minority opinions, stressed that if "there be a time to expose through discussion the falsehood and fallacies, to avert the evil by the processes of education, the remedy to be applied is more speech, not enforced silence."

Their views were not shared by Mr. Justice Sanford, another justice of the Supreme Court of the United States. He could not accept that freedom of the press conferred "an absolute right to speak or publish, without responsibility whatever one may choose." As far as he was concerned, an "unrestricted or unbridled license that gives immunity for every possible use of language ... prevents the punishment of those who abuse this freedom."

The dilemma posed by these two opposing views faced the United States Court of Appeal for the Seventh Circuit in *Village of Skokie v. Nationalist Socialist Party of America* in 1978. Frank Collin, the leader of the American Nazi Party wanted to hold a rally and had chosen the village of Skokie, a suburb of Chicago because its 600 residents were 40 per cent Jewish. The residents, some of whom were survivors of the concentration camps, were not prepared to allow the swastika, a symbol of so much pain and suffering in their lives, to be paraded defiantly in their village.

The members of the village moved quickly to obtain an injunction and were granted it on the grounds that a Nazi rally might incite the local residents to violence. The village council then passed three by-laws: the first required anyone holding a rally to post a $350,000 insurance bond; the second made it a crime in Skokie to distribute any material which "promotes and incites hatred against persons by reason of their race, national origin or religion"; and the third prohibited any public demonstration by a person wearing a military-style uniform.

Collin immediately applied for an order declaring the by-laws unconstitutional because they had the effect of preventing his constitutional right to freedom of speech and peaceable assembly. Judge Decker of the Federal District Court was forced to agree:

> In this case, a small group of zealots, openly professing to be followers of Nazism, have succeeded in exacerbating the emotions of a large segment of the citizens of the Village of Skokie who are bitterly opposed to their views and revolted by the prospect of their public appearance.
> When feelings and tensions are at their highest peak, it is a temptation to reach for the exception to the rule announced by Mr. Justice Holmes, "if there is any principle of the Constitution that more imperatively calls for attachment than any other it is the

principle of free thought — not free thought for those who agree with us but freedom for the thought we hate."

Freedom of thought carries with it the freedom to speak and to publicly assemble to express one's thoughts.

The long list of cases reviewed in this opinion agreed that when a choice must be made, it is better to allow those who preach racial hate to expend their venom in rhetoric rather than to be panicked into embarking on the dangerous course of permitting the government to decide what its citizens may say and hear.

## Canada Before the Charter

Before the enactment of the Charter of Rights and Freedoms, even before the Bill of Rights, the courts had little authority to guarantee freedom of expression unless it arose as a question of legislative competence. In other words, the courts could only protect freedom of expression if either a provincial legislature or Parliament attempted to curtail it and in so doing exceeded one of the enumerated powers under the British North America Act.

The most famous example of this was the Padlock Law. This was a statute passed in 1937 by the province of Quebec known as "An Act to Protect the Province against Communistic Propaganda". Although it was said that the Act was passed to stop the spread of communism in Quebec, it was really an attempt to stop the proselytizing activities of the Jehovah's Witnesses, who had invaded the province in the mid-1930s with messianic zeal. The Act made it illegal for any person who owned or occupied a house in the province of Quebec to allow it to be used to propagate communism or bolshevism. The Act also made it a crime to publish or distribute any writing which tended to propagate communism or bolshevism. The Attorney General of Quebec, Maurice Duplessis, who was also the Premier, was given absolute power to close any house for a period of not more than one year "upon satisfactory proof" that that house had been used to propagate communism.

John Switzman was sued by his landlady, Freda Elbling, claiming that he had breached the Padlock Law. Her action was successful before the Quebec Superior Court and the Quebec Court of Appeal. But Switzman appealed the judgment to the Supreme Court of Canada who set it aside. It was the Court's view that the Padlock Law was unconstitutional because it really was legislation in respect of criminal law, a matter exclusively within the legislative competence of the Parliament of Canada, not the provincial legislatures. One of the judges, Mr. Justice Abbott, was prepared to go even further stating that the right to free speech was "essential to the working of a parliamentary democracy such as ours." Although to strike down this law the Court merely had to declare that no provincial legislature had the right to pass the laws, Mr. Justice Abbott went further:

Although it is not necessary, of course, to determine this question for the purposes of the present appeal, the Canadian constitution being declared to be similar in principle to that of the United Kingdom, I am also of opinion that as our constitutional Act now stands, Parliament itself could not abrogate this right of discussion and debate. The power of Parliament to limit it is, in my view, restricted to such powers as may be exercised under its exclusive legislative jurisdiction with respect to criminal law and to make laws for the peace, order and good government of the nation.

Even democratic nations recognize that, if their institutions are to survive, laws must be passed which suppress any persons or groups that advocate the use of force as a means of overthrowing those institutions. Canada's sedition laws are a far cry from those that terrorized Englishmen four centuries ago.

Section 62 of the Criminal Code makes it an indictable offence to speak seditious words, publish a seditious libel or be a party to a seditious conspiracy. Seditious words are words that express a seditious intention. A seditious intention means to teach or advocate the use of force as a means of accomplishing a governmental change within Canada, without the authority of law.

The Criminal Code, however, recognizes that every Canadian citizen is entitled to criticize the Crown, the governments of Canada and the provinces, Parliament, the provincial legislatures and the courts. Section 61 of the Criminal Code provides that "no person shall be deemed to have a seditious intention by reason only that he intends, in good faith . . ." to show the errors or defects of the government or of the courts.

It was not, however, until the decision of the Supreme Court of Canada in *Boucher v. The Queen* that the courts were prepared to recognize that there had to be an intention to incite acts of violence or public disorder before a person could be found guilty of seditious libel. During the First World War, and later during the Winnipeg General Strikes, the courts had applied a definition contained in the *Digest of the Criminal Law* written by an English Judge, Sir James Stephen. That definition made it a crime merely to bring into hatred or contempt or to incite dissatisfaction against the Crown or the Government.

The Stephen definition ignores the fact that the purpose of criticizing government is to show our discontent or dissatisfaction with it. This would mean that anybody who was dissatisfied with the workings of government and wanted to criticize it, short of advocating a forceful overthrow, was guilty of sedition.

Aime Boucher was dissatisfied with the way the Government of Quebec was treating Jehovah's Witnesses. Boucher, who owned a small farm just outside the community of St. Joseph De Beauce, was seen distributing copies of a pamphlet to several persons in St. Joseph on December 11, 1946. The pamphlet was published by the Watchtower Bible and Truth Society of Toronto. It consisted of four pages. The heading on the front page read: "Quebec's burning hate for God and Christ and Freedom is the shame of all of Canada." The article underneath was an invocation to calmness and reason in appraising the matters to be dealt with in support of the heading. The pamphlet went on to refer to vindictive persecution of Jehovah's Witnesses in Quebec and gave a detailed narrative of the specific incident. It charged that the Roman Catholic Church in Quebec was involved directly in the administration of justice and was the force behind the prosecutions. The pamphlet described it in this way:

> [The] force behind Quebec's suicidal hate is priest domination. Thousands of Quebec Catholics are so blinded by the priests that they think they serve God's cause in mobbing Jehovah's Witnesses.

There was also an attack upon the courts and the administration of justice:

> What of her judges that impose heavy fines and prison sentences against them (Jehovah's Witnesses) and heap abusive language upon them and deliberately follow a malicious policy of again and again postponing cases to tie up tens of thousands of dollars in exorbitant bails and keep hundreds of cases pending?

After reciting some examples the pamphlet went on:

> Why, Catholic domination of Quebec courts is so complete that in the courtrooms the imagery of the crucifix takes the place of the British Coat of Arms, which appears in other courts throughout the Dominion.

The pamphlet concluded with an appeal to the people of the province that, through the study of God's word and obedience to His commands, there might be brought about a "bounteous crop of the good fruits of love for Him and Christ and human freedom."

Boucher was charged with publishing a seditious libel by distributing copies of his pamphlet and was convicted by a jury of twelve Quebec residents. His conviction was upheld by the Quebec Court of Appeal; but in a majority decision of the Supreme Court of Canada, his conviction was quashed. It held that there was no evidence, either in the pamphlet or otherwise, upon which a jury, properly instructed, could have found him guilty of the offence charged.

Mr. Justice Rand, who delivered an eloquent judgment, traced the law of sedition and then pointed out:

> Up to the end of the 18th century it was, in essence, a contempt in words of political authority or the actions of authority. If we conceive of the governors of society as superior beings, exercising a divine mandate, by whom laws, institutions and administrations are given to men to be obeyed, who are, in short, beyond criticism, reflection or censure upon them or what they do implies either an equality with them or an accountability by them, both equally offensive. In that lay sedition by words and the libel was its written form.

However, he went on to note that,

> But constitutional conceptions of a different order making rapid progress in the 19th century have necessitated a modification of the legal view of public criticism; and the administrators of what we call democratic government have come to be looked upon as servants, bound to carry out their duties accountably to the public. The basic nature of the Common-Law lies in its flexible process of traditional reasoning upon significant social and political matter; and just as in the 17th century the crime of seditious libel was a deduction from fundamental conceptions of government, the substitution of new conceptions, under the same principle of reasoning, called for new jural conclusions.

Then he pointed out:

> There is no modern authority which holds that mere effect of tending to create discontent or dissatisfaction among His Majesty's subjects or ill-will or hostility between groups of them, but not tending to issue in illegal conduct, constitutes the crime, and this for obvious reasons. Freedom in thought and speech and disagreement in ideas and beliefs, on every conceivable subject, are of the essence of our life. The clash of critical discussion on political, social and religious subjects has too deeply become the stuff of daily experience to suggest that mere ill-will as a product of controversy can strike down the latter with illegality. A superficial examination of the words shows its insufficiency: what is the degree necessary to criminality? Can it ever, as mere subjective condition, be so? Controversial fury is aroused constantly by differences in abstract conceptions; heresy in some fields is again a mortal sin; there can be fanatical puritanism in ideas as well as in mortals; but our compact of free society accepts and absorbs these differences and they are exercised at large within the framework of freedom and order on broader and deeper uniformities as bases of social stability. Similarly in discontent, affection and hostility: as subjective incidents of controversy, they and the ideas which arouse them are part of our living which ultimately serve us in stimulation, in the clarification of thought and, as we believe, in the search for the constitution and truth of things generally.

## Freedom of Expression Under the Charter

The last 25 years have witnessed a dramatic change in Canada's racial mosaic. It is no longer a country predominantly Anglo-Saxon in origin. Immigration since the Second World War has brought to Canada people of various races, religions and cultures from all over the world. The inevitable and unfortunate result has been a rising increase in the expression of racial prejudice.

Can racial prejudice, born and nurtured in ignorance, be stamped out by legal proscriptions? The Parliament of Canada obviously felt so when it enacted sections 281.1 and 281.2 of the Criminal Code in 1970.

Section 281.1 makes it a criminal offence to advocate or promote genocide. Section 281.2 makes it a criminal offence to communicate statements in any public place which incite hatred against any identifiable group where such incitement is likely to lead to a breach of the peace. The section also makes it an offence to communicate statements other than in private conversation which wilfully promote hatred against any identifiable group. However, section 281.2(3) protects such a person if he establishes that the statements communicated were true or made in good faith to establish by argument an opinion upon a religious subject or if the statements were for the public benefit.

Section 177 of the Criminal Code also makes it a criminal offence to wilfully publish a statement, tale or news that is known to be false and "that causes or is likely to cause injury or mischief to a public interest." It was this offence that Sabina Citron accused Ernst Zundel of committing when he published two pamphlets, the first "The West, War and Islam" and the second "Did Six Million Really Die?", when she appeared before a justice of the peace to lay an information against him.

The first pamphlet declared that an international conspiracy existed amongst Jews, Freemasons, bankers and Communists; its purpose promotion of Zionism and the domination of the world. Another suggested aim was the unification of western nations in an effort to dominate and subdue Islamic countries. The second pamphlet argued that the Holocaust — the deliberate extermination of six million European Jews by the Nazi Government in Germany and the nations under its control — was merely a hoax perpetrated by world Jewry to extort money from the German Government, and the German people, in order to promote Zionist interests. Although the pamphlet conceded that hundreds of thousands of Jews did die during the Second World War, it argued that this was the inevitable result of war; it was not a systematic attempt to exterminate European Jews.

The consent of the Attorney General of Ontario is required in order to launch a prosecution under section 281.1 and 281.2. Mrs. Citron had asked the Attorney General of Ontario to grant his consent to a prosecution under these sections but he had refused because he did not believe that a prosecution would succeed. Mrs. Citron, the head of the Holocaust Remembrance Association, turned to section 177 because the consent of the Attorney General is not necessary and launched a private prosecution. Eventually the Attorney General of Ontario intervened and assigned a special prosecutor to prosecute Ernst Zundel.

In Toronto, in the spring of 1985, Ernst Zundel was tried by Judge Locke of the District Court with a jury. The 46-year-old Toronto publisher did not deny publishing the pamphlets but argued that the statements were true. He also said that his purpose was to reveal the truth to the world for the public good. After a trial lasting several weeks, the jury accepted his explanation with respect to the first publication but rejected it on the second and convicted him. One could hardly have expected a different result. Attempts by a number of people to deny the existence of the Holocaust have not been convincing in view of the well documented and irrefutable evidence. Judge Locke sentenced Zundel to 15 months' imprisonment and ordered him not to discuss the Holocaust in any public communication for a period of three years.

Shortly after the completion of the Zundel trial another prosecution took place almost 2,000 miles to the west in Red Deer, Alberta. James Keegstra, a 51-year-old Christian Fundamentalist of Dutch descent, taught social studies from 1978 to 1982 at a high school in Eckville, a small farming community in central Alberta. He taught his students that the French revolution was "imported" by a secret Jewish sect called the Illuminati. His students were also told that Nazis used gas chambers in their concentration camps only for delousing and not extermination; the Nuremberg War Crimes Trials, he told them, were a miscarriage of justice because they were dominated by retribution and revenge rather than justice.

Keegstra, who had also been the mayor of Eckville, was forced to resign in 1982 when parents of the students complained to the school board. Shortly thereafter he was charged with wilfully promoting hatred against Jews, contrary to section 281.2 of the Criminal Code.

Twenty-three former students testified for the Crown that Keegstra awarded high marks for answers which expressed anti-Jewish opinions. Keegstra, in his defence, told the jury that he believed that a diabolical group of international financiers and atheistical Jews was conspiring to control the world and destroy Christianity. To support his views, he gave his own interpretation of world events which significantly departed from views generally held. He denied that there was any intention to promote hatred against Jews. Rather, he maintained that he was only trying to instill truth and knowledge in his students.

A jury of ten men and two women disagreed and convicted Keegstra. Mr. Justice MacKenzie, the presiding judge, concluded that jail was not the answer and fined him $500.

Before his trial, Keegstra had brought an application to stay the prosecution against him because section 281.2(2) of the Code infringed his right to "freedom of thought, belief, opinion and expression." Mr. Justice Quigley of the Alberta Queen's Bench heard the application and rejected it. It was his view that,

> [T]he wilful promotion of hatred under circumstances which fall within s. 281.2(2) of the *Criminal Code* of Canada clearly contradicts the principles which recognize the dignity and worth of the members of identifiable groups, singly and collectively; it contradicts the recognition of moral and spiritual values which impels us to assert and protect the dignity of each member of society; and it negates or limits the rights and freedoms of such target groups, and in particular denies them the right to the equal protection and benefit of the law without discrimination.
>
> Under these circumstances, it is my opinion that s. 281.2(2) of the *Code* cannot rationally be considered to be an infringement which limits "freedom of expression", but on the contrary it is a safeguard which promotes it. The protection afforded by the proscription tends to banish the apprehension which might otherwise inhibit certain segments of our society from freely expressing themselves upon the whole spectrum of

topics, whether social, economic, scientific, political, religious, or spiritual in nature. The unfettered right to express divergent opinions on these topics is the kind of freedom of expression the Charter protects.

As far as he was concerned, "freedom of expression" in the Charter did not mean an absolute freedom permitting an unabridged right of speech or expression.

Both Zundel and Keegstra have appealed their convictions because they contend that their constitutional guarantee of freedom of expression was denied them. In due course, the Supreme Court of Canada will have to consider whether freedom of expression does mean absolute and unabridged right of speech and expression. If it does not, then it will be necessary for the Court to decide how far the government may go to curtail freedom of speech which is directed towards fomenting hatred against others.

# 4

# Freedom of the Press and Other Media of Communication

The liberty of the press is dear to England. The licentiousness of the press is odious to England. The liberty of it can never be so well protected as by beating down the licentiousness. . . . I said that the liberty of the press was dear to Englishmen, and I will say that nothing can put that in danger but licentiousness of the press. . . . It is neither more nor less than this, that a man may publish anything which twelve of his countrymen think is not blamable, but that he ought to be punished if he publishes that which is blamable.

Lord Kenyon, *R. v. Cuthill* (1799)

If the words were of such a nature and were used under such circumstances that men, judging in calmness, could not reasonably say that they created a clear and present danger that they would bring about the evil that Congress sought and had a right to prevent, then it is the duty of the trial judge to withdraw the case from consideration by the jury; if he fails to do so, it is the duty of the appellate court to correct the error.

Mr. Justice Brandeis, *Schaefer v. United States* (1920)

The Moving Finger writes; and having writ,
Moves on: nor all thy Piety nor Wit
Shall lure it back to cancel half a Line,
Nor all thy Tears wash out a Word of it.

Rubaiyat of Omar Khayyam of Naishapur
(Translated by Edward Fitz Gerald)

Junius described the liberty of the press in 1769 as "The Palladium of all the civil, political and religious rights of an Englishman." Although the printing press had been invented by Johann Gutenberg in Germany in 1440, the first press was not established in England until 1476. Before his death in 1491, William Caxton, the first English printer, is believed to have published almost every important literary work written in English.

Long before the introduction of the printing press, English Kings recognized the need to suppress defamatory attacks upon their dignity and that of the other important members of their Kingdom. The earliest recorded statute known as "De Scandalis Magnatum" was passed in 1275 by Edward I. It provided that:

> Forasmuch as there have been oftentimes found in the country of tales whereby discord
> or occasion of discord has many times arisen between the king and his people or great
> men of this realm, for the damage that hath and may therefore ensue, it is commanded
> that from henceforth none be so hardy to cite or publish any false news or tales whereby
> discord or occasion of discord or slander may grow between the king and his people or
> the great men of the realm; and he that doth so shall be taken and kept in prison until he
> hath brought him into court which was the first author of the tale.

The printing press, however, soon created a new problem for the Crown. Dissension and sedition could now be spread quickly from one end of the country to the other with anonymity. The Court of Star Chamber, created by an Act of Parliament in 1487 during the reign of Henry VII, now began to take over the administration of the statute De Scandalis Magnatum, which had been extended earlier to include peers, prelates, justices and various other officials within its protection.

To control printing and publishing, the Star Chamber introduced a system of censorship. Ordinances were passed which required a special licence to print a book. The ordinances also regulated the manner of printing and the number of presses that were allowed to operate. Established during the reign of Queen Mary, the Stationers' Company, composed of 97 London Stationers, was granted a monopoly over printing. This company was also given the power to seize any publication by an outsider and to bring the offender before the Star Chamber.

To ensure that there was not the slightest criticism of the monarch or officials of the Crown, the Star Chamber developed the law of seditious libel in 1606 in the case *De Libellis Famosis*. The law was based on the theory that a seditious libel against the Crown and its officials imperilled the security of the state. The Star Chamber was also concerned that a libel upon a private person might cause a breach of the peace because the honourable way to defend a reputation was by dueling. Thus, the law of libel was extended to private persons although it was not considered as serious as

> ... (I)f it be against a magistrate or other public person ... for it concerns not only the
> breach of the peace, but also the scandal of government; for what greater scandal of
> government can there be than to have corrupt or wicked magistrates to be appointed
> and constituted by the King to govern his subjects under him? And greater imputation
> to the state cannot be, than to suffer such corrupt men to sit in the sacred seat of justice,
> or to have any meddling in or concern in the administration of justice.

Seditious libels were punished severely by the Court of Star Chamber. Although only the common law courts could pass the death penalty, the Star Chamber found other methods to suppress seditious libels.

The abolition of the Star Chamber by the Long Parliament in 1641 did not bring an end to the licensing system. The Long Parliament introduced its own licensing system in 1642 which was revived after the Restoration by the Licensing Act of 1662 and did not lapse until 1695. During this period the common law courts began to assume jurisdiction over the offence of libel. Judges, who were generally more sympathetic to the Crown, were concerned that juries might be too ready to acquit where the criticism was justified. To control their verdict, the judges developed a rule stating that the jury was required only to decide if the accused had published the writing. Whether the writing was seditious or not was a question of law — a question to be decided only by the trial judge, usually after the verdict had been rendered. Nor was it any defence that the article was true. Juries were therefore directed by the trial judge to return a verdict of guilty if they were satisfied that the accused had published the article in question.

William Shipley became the Dean of St. Asaph after the death of his father, Dr. Jonathon Shipley. At 22, he had married an heiress which permitted him to enjoy an active social life as well as a religious one. Notwithstanding the privilege which he enjoyed, the Dean had developed a genuine interest in the welfare of his fellow man. In 1782, he printed a political pamphlet which had been written by his brother-in-law, Sir William Jones. Entitled "The Principles of Government in a Dialogue Between a Gentleman and a Farmer", it expressed the opinion that every man of 21 had the right to vote and to send representatives to Parliament. At the instigation of the sheriff of the county, a grand jury returned a bill of indictment charging him with "being a person of wicked and turbulent disposition . . . and to diffuse among the subjects of the realm discontents, jealousies, and suspicions of our lord the King and his government . . . and to incite the subjects . . . by force and violence and with arms to make alteration in the government . . . he had seditiously published a false, wicked, malicious, seditious and scandalous libel of and concerning our said lord the King and the government of this realm in the form of a supposed dialogue between a supposed gentleman and a supposed farmer. . . ."

Thomas Erskine, later to become Lord Chancellor of England was retained to defend the Dean. Born in 1750, he did not begin to study law until he was 25. Three years later in 1778, he was called to the Bar, penniless, and without influential friends. Nevertheless, within a few years he became the greatest lawyer in all of England and the staunchest defender of the jury system.

The trial of the Dean of St. Asaph began in August 1784. The presiding judge was Mr. Justice Buller. Erskine knew Buller for he had been his pupil while a student. He also knew Buller would instruct the jury that their duty was to decide only if the Dean of St. Asaph had published the pamphlet.

After the Crown presented evidence to establish that the Dean had published the article, Erskine rose to address the jury. He spoke to them for almost three hours.

> A jury are no more forced to return a special verdict in cases of libel than upon other trials criminal and civil where law is mixed with fact. . . Say the contrary who will, I

assert this to be the genuine, unrepealed constitution of England; and therefore if the learned judge shall tell you that this pamphlet is in the abstract a libel . . . I shall not agree that you are therefore bound to find the defendant guilty unless you think so likewise. . . . Crimes consist wholly in intention. Of that which passes in the breast of an Englishman as the motives of his action, none but an English jury shall judge. . . . The administration of criminal justice in the hands of the people is the basis of freedom. While that remains there can be no tyranny, because the people will not execute tyrannical laws on themselves. Whenever it is lost, liberty must fall along with it, because the sword of justice falls into the hands of men who, however independent, have no common interest with the mass of the people. Our whole history is therefore checkered with the struggle of our ancestors to maintain this important privilege, which in cases of libel has been too often a shameful and disgraceful subject of controversy.

He concluded:

Let me conclude with reminding you, gentlemen, that if you find the defendant guilty, not believing the thing published to be a libel, or the intention of the publisher sedition, your verdict and your opinion will be at variance. And it will then be between God and your own conscience to reconcile the contradiction.

After the jury were instructed by Mr. Justice Buller, they retired. They returned within one half hour. The clerk of the court rose and asked the jury if they found the defendant guilty or not guilty. The reply caused the courtroom to buzz with excitement. "We find him guilty of publishing only."

But Mr. Justice Buller was not prepared to accept such a verdict. He addressed the jury: "I believe that is a verdict not quite correct. You must explain that one way or the other as to the meaning of the innuendoes. The indictment has stated that " 'G' means Gentlemen, 'F' Farmer, the 'King', the King of Great Britain, and the 'Parliament', the Parliament of Great Britain."

One of the jurors replied "we have no doubt of that."

Mr. Justice Buller now insisted: "If you find him guilty of publishing, you must not say the word *only*."

Erskine was concerned that this might intimidate the jury and interjected "By that they mean to find that there was no sedition."

Several members agreed and responded: "We only find him guilty of publishing. We do not find anything else. Certainly, that is all we do find."

After further discussion, Erskine insisted: "My Lord, I desire the verdict may be recorded. I desire Your Lordship sitting here as a judge, to record the verdict as given by the jury. If the jury departs from the word 'only', they alter their verdict."

Mr. Justice Buller again addressed the jury trying to get them to agree that they meant to find the Dean guilty of publishing the libel. When it appeared that the jury were about to agree to this wording, Erskine interrupted "Is the word 'only' to stand as part of your verdict?"

When a member of the jury replied "certainly", Erskine turned to the judge: "Then I insist that it shall be recorded."

This resulted in the now famous confrontation between the two:

BULLER J: Then the verdict must be misunderstood. Let me understand the jury.

ERSKINE: The jury do understand their verdict.

BULLER J: Sir, I will not be interrupted.

ERSKINE: I stand here as an advocate for a brother citizen. I desire the word "only" to be recorded.

BULLER J: Sit down sir. Remember your duty, or I shall be obliged to proceed in another manner.

Erskine knew that this was a threat to punish him for contempt of court. But this threat did not stop him from doing what he knew to be his duty.

Your Lordship may proceed in what manner you think fit; I know my duty as well as Your Lordship knows yours. I shall not alter my conduct.

Eventually after further discussion between the judge, the jury and with Erskine pressing his point, the verdict was finally recorded. It read: "Guilty of publishing, but whether of libel or not, we do not find."

Three months later, Erskine appeared before the Court of King's Bench to ask for a new trial. Presiding was Lord Mansfield, the Chief Justice of England. Almost 80, he had been Chief Justice for nearly 30 years. Mansfield had not only presided as a judge in many libel cases, he had also prosecuted some when he was Attorney General of England. In every case as the trial judge, he had instructed the jury to return a verdict of guilty if it was established that the accused had published the article in question.

The trial, however, had received much publicity in England. From every quarter, there was criticism of the decision. Erskine's colleague in Parliament, Charles James Fox had found the impetus to introduce a bill to change the law. But although the bill was introduced in 1784 in the House of Commons, it was held up in the House of Lords for eight years by Chancellor Thurlow. Fox's bill finally became law in 1792.

It provided that upon the trial of an indictment or information for libel, "the jury sworn to try the issue may give a general verdict of guilty or not guilty . . . and shall not be required or directed by the court or judge . . . to find the defendant . . . guilty, merely on proof of the publication of the paper charged to be a libel, and of the sense ascribed to the same in the indictment or information."

However, it took another 50 years before other defects in the libel laws disappeared. As noted earlier, truth had never been a defence to the crime of libel. Furthermore, an employer was considered responsible if his employee published a libel. In 1843, Lord Campbell's Act was passed. It provided that an accused was to be acquitted if he could prove that the libel was true and for the public benefit. It also exempted an employer from criminal responsibility for a libel published by his employee, if he could prove that it was done without consent, knowledge or authority, and without a lack of due care on his part.

## The Colonies Rebel Against the Common Law

The new settlers in the colonies enjoyed no greater freedom of the press than they did in England. A licensing system was quickly introduced which censored any publication thought to be dangerous to the Crown.

The most famous libel trial during this period took place in 1735. Peter Zenger, the publisher of *The New York Weekly Journal* had published satirical ballads reflecting on the Governor and his Council. When the grand jury refused to indict Zenger, the Governor directed his Attorney General to file an information. The information described the ballads "as having in them many things tending to raise factions and tumults among the people of this provence, inflaming their minds with contempt for his majesty's government, and greatly disturbing the peace thereof."

Zenger's defence got off to a bad start when his counsel were disbarred for having the audacity to question the Chief Justice's right to preside in the trial. When Andrew Hamilton, a Quaker lawyer from Philadelphia offered to defend Zenger, he quickly accepted. Hamilton conceded at the outset of the trial that Zenger had published the ballads but asked to be allowed to prove that the matters contained in them were true. The Chief Justice, however, refused: "A libel is not to be justified; for it is nevertheless a libel that it is true."

Hamilton then urged that the jury be allowed to give a general verdict. Again the Chief Justice refused just as Mr. Justice Buller was to refuse Erskine almost 50 years later,

> No, Mr. Hamilton; the jury may find that Mr. Zenger printed and published these papers, and leave it to the Court to judge whether they are libellous. You know this is very common: it is in the nature of a Special Verdict, where the jury leave the matter of law to the Court.

Hamilton, however, appealed to the jury just as Erskine was to do and the jury returned a verdict of not guilty. The feat was described as "a generous defence of the rights of mankind, and the liberty of the press."

It was in this atmosphere, in 1776, that the First Congress of the thirteen states met to hammer out a constitution. Initially, it was felt that a bill of rights was not necessary to protect the citizens of the new United States. A declaration which asserted that "all men are created equal, that they are endowed by their Creator with certain unalienable Rights, that among these are Life, Liberty and the pursuit of Happiness" was a sufficient protection. Some, such as Alexander Hamilton even felt that a bill of rights had no place in a constitution which recognized sovereignty in the people.

However, over the next decade, agitation for a bill of rights emerged from every segment of society. Finally in 1791, first ten amendments were adopted by Congress and approved by the states. The First Amendment provided that,

Congress shall make no law respecting . . .
. . . abridging the freedom of speech, or of the press;

## Sedition in America

Ironically within ten years of the adoption of the First Amendment, Congress passed the Alien and Sedition Laws. The Sedition Act made it an offence for anyone to "write, print, utter or publish . . . any false, scandalous and malicious writing or writings against the Government of the United States, or the President of the United States" with intent to defame them or bring them into contempt or disrepute or to excite against them the hatred "of the good people of the United States." An accused, however, was entitled to prove the truth of the publication and the jury could determine not only whether he published it but whether it was defamatory in nature. The Sedition Act had been passed by Congress because of the fear of a war with France which was to happen shortly thereafter. A number of successful prosecutions followed between 1798 and 1801.

Although the Act, unlike the English law, made truth admissible as evidence in defence, judges who presided over the trials insisted that the entire truth of the matter be proved by a single witness. This had the practical effect of perpetuating the English law of sedition for another century. It was not until 1931 that the first broadside was levelled by Chief Justice Hughes of the Supreme Court of the United States in *Near v. Minnesota*. There he wrote:

The exceptional nature of its limitations places in a strong light the general conception that liberty of the press, historically considered and taken by the Federal Constitution, has meant, principally although not exclusively, immunity from previous restraints or censorship. The conception of the liberty of the press in this country had broadened with the exigencies of the colonial period and with the efforts to secure freedom from oppressive administration.

The death knell was finally sounded by the Supreme Court of the United States five years later in *Grosgean v. American Press Co.* by Mr. Justice Sutherland:

It is impossible to concede that by the words "freedom of the press" the framers of the amendment intended to adopt merely the narrow view then reflected by the law of England that such freedom consisted only in immunity from previous censorship; for this abuse had then permanently disappeared from British practice. . . . Undoubtedly, the range of a constitutional provision phrased in terms of the common law sometimes may be fixed by recourse to the applicable rules of that law. But the doctrine which justifies such recourse, like other canons of construction, must yield to more compelling reasons whenever they exist. . . . And, obviously, it is subject to the qualification that the common law rule invoked shall be one not rejected by our ancestors as unsuited to their civil or political conditions.

## Liberty of the Press in Canada

The common law of England, and along with it the law of seditious libel, was introduced into the original Canadian provinces, with the exception of Quebec, before 1867. With the union of the provinces in 1867 into a Confederation, the Dominion Parliament was given exclusive jurisdiction over the criminal law. In 1892, the Criminal Code was enacted essentially along the lines of the English draft Criminal Code which the United Kingdom eventually rejected. The crime of seditious libel was now committed to a statutory definition which has remained unchanged over the last century. Section 262, the present revision, defines a defamatory libel as a "matter published, without lawful justification or excuse, that is likely to injure the reputation of any person by exposing him to hatred, contempt or ridicule, that is designed to insult the person of or concerning whom it is published."

The Criminal Code also provides defences to an accusation of libel which are patterned after those in Lord Campbell's Act and its Canadian successor, An Act respecting the Crime of Libel, introduced in the province of Canada in 1874. They include the publishing in good faith, for the information of the public, of a fair report of the proceedings of the Senate, the House of Commons or a legislature, or a committee thereof or any public judicial proceedings, including any fair comment upon the proceedings. Also protected is a fair and accurate report of the proceedings of any public meeting, if the publication is for the public benefit, as well as fair comments upon the public conduct of a person who takes part in public affairs. The most important defence of all is truth. Section 275 provides:

No person shall be deemed to publish a defamatory libel where he proves that the publication of the defamatory matter in the manner in which it was published was for the public benefit at the time when it was published and that the matter itself was true.

Section 2(*b*) of the Canadian Charter of Rights and Freedoms declares ". . . freedom of the press and other media of communication" as a fundamental freedom. Although truth of a publication is a protected defence to an accused under the Criminal Code, it is a defence which the accused must establish if he is to avoid a prosecution. This requirement appears to clash with the guarantee of freedom of the press and the presumption of innocence "until proven guilty" guaranteed to any person charged with an offence under section 11(*d*) of the Charter. Recent Canadian decisions indicate that any requirement by an accused to prove his innocence will be struck down if there is no connection between the proved fact and the presumed fact. It is very possible therefore that Canadian courts may in the future impose on the prosecution the obligation to establish that a publication was not true.

The last century has witnessed few prosecutions in Canada of defamatory libel. This is probably due to the belief that such prosecutions should only be undertaken when there is a risk of a breach of the peace or where it seriously affects the reputation of the person defamed. Indeed, the Law Reform Commission of Canada has recommended that libel be abolished as a crime, since anyone affected can pursue his remedy by a civil action for libel or defamation.

Almost 50 years ago, the province of Alberta passed a statute known as "An Act to Ensure the Publication of Accurate News and Information", designed to censor the press from publishing statements which would attack the policies of the Social Credit Party, then in power. In ruling that the statute was *ultra vires* the provinces because it was part of the Alberta Social Credit Act, an Act dealing with banks and banking and therefore a matter solely within the exclusive domain of the federal Parliament, Mr. Justice Cannon of the Supreme Court of Canada reminded us:

> Under the British system, which is ours, no political party can erect a prohibitory barrier to prevent the electors from getting information concerning the policy of the government. Freedom of discussion is essential to enlighten public opinion in a democratic State; it cannot be curtailed without affecting the right of the people to be informed through sources independent of the government concerning matters of public interest. There must be an untramelled publication of the news and political opinions of the political parties contending for ascendancy. As stated in the preamble of *The British North America Act*, our constitution is and will remain, unless radically changed, "similar in principle to that of the United Kingdom." At the time of Confederation, the United Kingdom was a democracy. Democracy cannot be maintained without its foundation: free public opinion and free discussion throughout the nation of all matters affecting the State within the limits set by the criminal code and the common law.

# 5

# Freedom From Arbitrary Detention or Imprisonment

If the Japs are released no one will be able to tell a saboteur from any other Jap.

Earl Warren, Governor of the State of California, (1943)

I have since deeply regretted the Removal Order and my own testimony advocating it, because it was not in keeping with our American concept of freedom and the rights of citizens . . . it was wrong to react so impulsively, without positive evidence of disloyalty, even though we felt we had good motive in the security of our state.

Earl Warren, Chief Justice of the United States
in his memoirs

Few men are aroused by injustice when they are sure of not being its victims . . . when authority in any form bullies a man unfairly, all other men are guilty; for it is their tacit assent that allows authority to commit the abuse.

Pierre Elliott Trudeau, Vrai (1958)

I think society must take every means at its disposal to defend itself against the emergence of parallel power which defies the elected power in this country, and I think that goes to any distance. So long as there is a power in here which is challenging the elected representatives of the people, I think that power must be stopped and I think it is only . . . weak-kneed bleeding hearts who are afraid to take these measures.

Prime Minister Trudeau — CBC broadcast,
October 13, 1970

On December 7, 1941, the Japanese Air Force dropped bombs on the American naval base at Pearl Harbour. Although some believed that war between the United States and Japan could be averted by diplomatic means, most knew that it was inevitable. The attack on Pearl Harbour and the subsequent declaration of war by the United States against the Japanese Empire ignited public hysteria against all Americans of Japanese origin. Anti-Japanese and anti-Chinese agitation was not new in America, particularly in California where over 80 percent of the ethnic Japanese population resided. But now it was no longer restricted to white-supremacy groups and some politicians who had used the fear of the Japanese menace to advance their careers. Newspapers along the west coast printed virulent racist editorials that incited outrage among white Californians against their Japanese-American neighbours. Government propaganda, supported by the press, conjured up a stereotype of a Japanese person in the American public eye. According to an American public opinion poll, the Japanese were considered treacherous, sly, cruel and war-like.

The day after the attack on Pearl Harbour, the United States Congress declared war against Japan. On February 19, 1942, the President of the United States, Franklin D. Roosevelt proclaimed Executive Order Number 9066 which recited that "Successful prosecution of the war requires every possible protection against espionage and against sabotage to national-defence material, national-defence premises, national-defence utilities." An order was issued authorizing the Secretary of War to designate certain areas in the United States as "Military Areas." Military commanders in those areas were given the discretion to exclude "potential enemies" from those areas.

The next day, Lieutenant General DeWitt was named as Military Commander of the Western Defence Command which comprised the western most states (about one fourth of the total area of the United States). On March 2, 1942 he issued a proclamation reciting that the entire Pacific coast "by its geographical location is particularly subject to attack, to attempted invasion by the armed forces of nations with which the United States is now at war, and, in connection therewith, is subject to espionage and acts of sabotage, thereby requiring the adoption of military measures necessary to establish safeguards against such enemy operations." Two military zones were designated. Military Area Number 1 embraced all of the coastal region of the three Pacific coast states and southern Arizona. Military Area Number 2 designated those areas not covered by Military Area Number 1. On March 21, 1942, Congress followed suit by passing a law making it a misdemeanour to disobey orders issued by the Military Commander.

On March 24, 1942, General De Witt issued a proclamation declaring that "all alien Japanese, all alien Germans, all alien Italians, *and all persons of Japanese ancestry*" residing or being within the geographical limits of Military Area Number 1 . . . shall be within their place of residence between the hours of 8:00 p.m. and 6:00 a.m. This proclamation was followed by further ones restricting "all alien Japanese and persons of Japanese ancestry" from leaving the area in which they resided. Finally on May 3, 1942 General DeWitt issued "Civilian Exclusion Order Number 34" which provided that "after 12:00 o'clock May 8th, 1942, all persons of Japanese ancestry, both alien and non-alien, 'were to be excluded from Military Area Number 1.'" It required a responsible member of each family to report for instructions to go to an assembly centre. Anyone who failed to do so was liable to prosecution. The obvious purpose of the order, to use the words of Mr. Justice Roberts of the United States Supreme Court, "was to drive all persons of Japanese ancestry into assembly centres within the zones of their residence, under pain of criminal prosecution." The ultimate goal was to force all Americans of Japanese ancestry into permanent detention camps for the duration of the war.

The result of this order was that in the months to follow, over 100,000 Japanese-Americans living along the west coast of the United States were arrested and relocated in other parts of the United States. No attempt was made to distinguish between loyal and disloyal Japanese-Americans, or between citizens and aliens. General DeWitt, himself, speaking before the House Naval Affairs sub-committee to investigate congested areas said,

> I don't want any of them (persons of Japanese ancestry) here. They are a dangerous element. There is no way to determine their loyalty. The west coast contains too many vital installations essential to the defence of the country to allow any Japanese on this coast . . . the danger of the Japanese was, and is now — if they are permitted to come back — espionage and sabotage. It makes no difference whether he is an American citizen, he is still a Japanese. American citizenship does not necessarily determine loyalty . . . but we must worry about the Japanese all the time until he is wiped off the map. Sabotage and espionage will make problems as long as he is allowed in this area. . . .

General DeWitt had no evidence to support these serious allegations. In fact, he could not point to one instance of an act of sabotage by any American of Japanese ancestry to support his allegations of disloyalty. However that did not deter him. On February 14, 1942, speaking before the committee, he stated that "the very fact that no sabotage has taken place to date is a disturbing and confirming indication that such action will be taken." He was supported by Earl Warren, then California State Attorney General, who told the committee that to believe the absence of sabotage by the Japanese population was proof of loyalty was "simply to live in a fool's paradise."

Few voices were raised in opposition to what was later described by Senator Sam J. Ervin as "the single most blatant violation of the Constitution in our history." The attitude of the American public was best reflected in a statement by the Governor of Idaho who said "the Japs live like rats, breed like rats and act like rats." The result was American citizens of Japanese ancestry suffered loss of liberty and dignity. Many also faced financial ruin as their homes and properties were sold, often for a pittance.

The cases of three young American citizens of Japanese ancestry, who decided to challenge the orders of General DeWitt, eventually reached the

Supreme Court of the United States. The first was that of Kiyoshi Hirabayashi. He was a 24-year-old senior at the University of Washington who
had been born in Seattle in 1918. His parents had come from Japan a few
years before and had never returned. Kiyoshi was educated in the Washington public schools and had never been in Japan or had any association with
Japanese residing there. He refused to report to the civil control station on
May 11 and 12, 1942, as directed, to register for evacuation from the
military area. He admitted doing so because he believed that if he did he
would be waiving his rights as an American citizen. He also admitted being
away from his place of residence after 8:00 p.m. on May 9, 1942 in contra-
vention of the curfew. He was charged and convicted of both offences and
sentenced to imprisonment for three months. He appealed his conviction,
arguing that his Fifth Amendment right not to be "deprived of life, liberty,
or property, without due process of law" had been taken away. He did not
deny that a curfew was an appropriate step taken by the government
against potential sabotage. However, he argued that it was unconstitutional because it was only directed to Americans of Japanese ancestry. A
unanimous nine member Supreme Court of the United States did not agree.
Chief Justice Stone summed up the Court's view in these words:

> Distinctions between citizens solely because of their ancestry are by their very nature
> odious to a free people whose institutions are founded upon the doctrine of equality.
> For that reason, legislative classification or discrimination based on race alone has often
> been held to be a denial of equal protection. . . . We may assume that these considera-
> tions would be controlling here were it not for the fact that the danger of espionage and
> sabotage, in time of war and of threatened invasion, calls upon the military authorities
> to scrutinize every relevant fact bearing on the loyalty of populations in the danger
> areas. Because racial discriminations are in most circumstances irrelevant and therefore
> prohibited, it by no means follows that, in dealing with the perils of war, Congress and
> the Executive are wholly precluded from taking into account those facts and circum-
> stances which are relevant to measures for our national defence and for the successful
> prosecution of the war, and which may in fact place citizens of one ancestry in a different
> category from others. . . . The adoption by Government, in the crisis of war and of
> threatened invasion, of measures for the public safety, based upon the recognition of
> facts and circumstances which indicate that a group of one national extraction may
> menace that safety more than others, is not wholly beyond the limits of the Constitution
> and is not to be condemned merely because in other and in most circumstances racial
> distinctions are irrelevant.

Relying upon reports of hearings held by Congress, he noted that,
generally, people of Japanese ancestry who had emigrated to the United
States in substantial numbers since the close of the last century had not
assimilated as an integral part of the white population, although he recognized that this was probably because there were strict laws and public
attitudes preventing them from doing so. He also noted that many children
of Japanese parentage were sent to Japanese language schools after regular
hours of public school in their locality. He assumed, without any evidence,

that some of these schools were the source of Japanese nationalistic propaganda which cultivated allegiance to Japan. Further, he observed that under Japanese law, all children born of parents with Japanese ancestry were entitled to claim Japanese citizenship. All of these factors, he argued, might have tended to increase the isolation of people of Japanese ancestry "and in many instances their attachment to Japan and its institutions." For these reasons, he concluded that Congress and the Executive, and all others charged with the responsibility for national events were entitled to take these factors into account in times of crisis:

> The Constitution as a continuously operating charter of government does not demand the impossible or the impractical. The essentials of the legislative function are preserved when Congress authorizes a statutory command to become operative, upon ascertainment of a basic conclusion of fact by a designated representative of the Government. . . . Under the Executive Order the basic facts, determined by the Military Commander in the light of knowledge when available, were whether that danger existed and whether a curfew order was an appropriate means of minimizing the danger. Since his findings to that effect were, as we have said, not without adequate support, the legislative function was performed and the sanction of the statute attached to violations of the curfew order.

A month after Kiyoshi Hirabayashi was charged with breaching the curfew, Toyosaburo Korematsu challenged the Civilian Exclusion Order issued by General DeWitt on May 8, 1942 excluding him from the County of Alameda, California. Korematsu was a resident of San Leandro in Alemeda County. He was born in the United States of Japanese ancestry; there was no suggestion that he had ever committed or was guilty of an act of disloyalty to the United States. But like others of similar ancestry, he found himself in a terrible predicament. One order issued by General DeWitt forbade him from leaving the zone in which he lived. Under another order, he was forbidden to be found within that zone unless he was in an assembly centre located in the zone. The assembly centre, to use the words of one judge, was "a euphemism for prison." The only way Korematsu could avoid punishment was to go to an assembly centre and submit himself to military imprisonment. He decided to do nothing.

On June 12, 1942 he was charged and convicted of breaching the exclusion order. Sentence was suspended and he was placed on probation for five years. However, the effect was that he was immediately taken into military custody and lodged in an assembly centre to be eventually moved to a relocation centre (or what that same judge called a concentration camp). He appealed his conviction and on December 18, 1944 the Supreme Court of the United States delivered its judgment.

Again, the Court upheld the Exclusion Order because it was directed towards the prevention of espionage and sabotage. It reaffirmed the principle that when a country, in a state of war, is threatened by hostile forces, it is entitled to protect itself by the use of power commensurate with threatened danger. Mr. Justice Black, who delivered the opinion of the Court, was not prepared to accept the suggestion that this was a case involving the imprisonment of a loyal citizen in a concentration camp because of racial prejudice. The issue was more simple than that:

> Korematsu was not excluded from the Military Area because of hostility to him or his race. He was excluded because we are at war with the Japanese Empire, because the properly constituted military authorities feared an invasion of our West Coast and felt constrained to take proper security measures, because they decided that the military urgency of the situation demanded that all citizens of Japanese ancestry be segregated from the West Coast temporarily; and finally because Congress, reposing its confidence in this time of war in our military leaders — as inevitably it must — determined that they should have the power to do just this. There was evidence of disloyalty on the part of some, the military authorities considered that the need for action was great, and time was short. We cannot — by availing ourselves of the calm prospective of hindsight — now say that at that time these actions were unjustified.

This time, however, three justices disagreed. Mr. Justice Murphy was prepared to concede that the military and naval situation in the spring of 1942 "was such as to generate a very real fear of invasion of the Pacific Coast, accompanied by fears of sabotage and espionage in that area." He was also prepared to accept that the Military Command was justified "in adopting all reasonable means necessary to combat those dangers." But as far as he was concerned,

> . . . the exclusion, either temporarily or permanently, of all persons with Japanese blood in their veins has no such reasonable relation. And that relation is lacking because the exclusion order necessarily must rely for its reasonableness upon the assumption that *all* persons of Japanese ancestry may have a dangerous tendency to commit sabotage and espionage and to aid our Japanese enemy in other ways. It is difficult to believe that reason, logic or experience could be marshalled in support of such an assumption.

He then went on to refer to General DeWitt's report, issued on June 5, 1943, which referred to individuals of Japanese descent as "subversive", as belonging to "an enemy race" whose "racial strains are undiluted" and as constituting "over 112,000 potential enemies . . . at large today" along the Pacific Coast and given to "emperor worshipping ceremonies." As far as he was concerned, these reports were "largely an accumulation of much of the misinformation, half-truths and insinuations that for years have been directed against Japanese Americans by people with racial and economic prejudices — the same people who have been among the foremost advocates of the evacuation." He also noted that not one person of Japanese ancestry had ever been accused or convicted of espionage or sabotage after Pearl Harbour while they were still free. He thus concluded:

> The military necessity which is essential to the validity of the evacuation order thus resolves itself into a few intimations that certain individuals actively aided the enemy, from which it is inferred that the entire group of Japanese Americans could not be

trusted to be or remain loyal to the United States. No one denies, of course, that there were some disloyal persons of Japanese descent on the Pacific Coast who did all in their power to aid their ancestral land. Similar disloyal activities have been engaged in by many persons of German, Italian and even more pioneer stock in our country. But to infer that examples of individual disloyalty proved group disloyalty and justified discriminatory action against the entire group is to deny that under our system of law individual guilt is the sole basis for deprivation of rights. Moreover, this inference which is at the very heart of the evacuation orders, has been used in support of the abhorrent and despicable treatment of minority groups by the dictatorial tyrannies which this nation is now pledged to destroy. To give constitutional sanction to that inference in this case, however well-intentioned may have been the military command on the Pacific coast, is to adopt one of the cruelest of the rationales used by our enemies to destroy the dignity of the individual and to encourage and open the door to discriminatory actions against other minority groups in the passions of tomorrow. . . .

I dissent, therefore, from this legalization of racism. Racial discrimination in any form and in any degree has no justifiable part whatever in our democratic way of life. It is unattractive in any setting but it is utterly revolting among a free people who have embraced the principles set forth in the Constitution of the United States. All residents of this nation are kin in some way by blood or culture to a foreign land. Yet they are primarily and necessarily a part of the new and distinct civilization of the United States. They must accordingly be treated at all times as the heirs of the American experiment and as entitled to all the rights and freedoms guaranteed by the Constitution.

Mitsuye Endo was evacuated from Sacramento, California in 1942, pursuant to one of General DeWitt's orders, and removed to the Tule Lake War Relocation Centre at Newell, Modoc County, California. She was also born in the United States of Japanese ancestry. In July 1942, she filed a petition for a writ of *habeas corpus* asking that she be discharged and her liberty restored. But her application was dismissed. In August of 1943 she was transferred to the Central Utah Relocation Centre in Topaz, Utah. She appealed the denial of her writ of *habeas corpus* and the matter was eventually heard by the Supreme Court of the United States 28 months later on October 12, 1944.

By this time, there was no longer any fear of a Japanese attack along the West Coast. The War Department and the military leadership in Washington had acknowledged a year earlier that there was no longer any military necessity in continuing the exclusion orders and maintaining the detention camps. However, President Roosevelt decided to ignore the recommendations and continue the policy.

In its argument before the Supreme Court on October 12, 1944 the Department of Justice conceded that Mitsuye Endo was a loyal and law abiding citizen and there was not the slightest suspicion of her disloyalty. They also conceded that there was no real reason why she should be detained any longer in the relocation centre. They maintained, however, that her detention for an additional period was an essential step in the ultimate plan of the government to resettle her and other detainees at the camps. It was argued that unless there was a planned and orderly resettlement, it might create "a dangerously disorderly migration of unwanted people to unprepared communities." It was argued that although community hostility had diminished towards the Japanese who had been evacuated, it had not disappeared. In other words, their continued detention and eventual resettlement was necessary for their own protection.

This time, the court unanimously agreed to grant *habeas corpus* and release Mitsuye Endo. Mr. Justice Douglas, who delivered the opinion of the Court, was careful to rest his judgment on the basis that the original exclusion order had never really authorized any detention of persons of Japanese ancestry but merely their relocation away from the Pacific coastal region. If they eventually found themselves detained in Relocation Centres, it was because of the hostility of the communities where they attempted to go. Since there was no longer any military necessity for their detention, and it was conceded that Mitsuye Endo was loyal, there was no reason to detain her any longer. Although Mr. Justice Murphy and Mr. Justice Roberts agreed with the result, they could not accept those reasons for her release. Mr. Justice Murphy put it this way:

> If, as I believe, the military orders excluding her from California were invalid at the time they were issued, they are increasingly objectionable at this late date, when the threat of invasion of the Pacific Coast and the fears of sabotage and espionage have greatly diminished. For the Government to suggest under these circumstances that the presence of Japanese blood in a loyal American citizen might be enough to warrant her exclusion from a place where she would otherwise have a right to go is a position I cannot sanction.

Mr. Justice Roberts agreed:

> I conclude, therefore, that the court is squarely faced with a serious constitutional question, whether the relator's detention violated the guarantees of the Bill of Rights of the federal Constitution and especially the guarantee of due process of law. There can be but one answer to that question. An admittedly loyal citizen has been deprived of her liberty for a period of years. Under the Constitution she should be free to come and go as she pleases. Instead, her liberty of motion and other innocent activities have been prohibited and conditioned. She should be discharged.

The judgment of the Supreme Court of the United States was delivered on December 18, 1944 releasing Mitsuye Endo from detention where she had been confined for over thirty months. Ironically the judgment was delivered one day after the War Relocation Authority officially declared that the detention camps were to close.

## Apprehended Insurrection in Canada

Canadians have no reason to feel proud of their treatment of Japanese Canadians during the Second World War. Not only were 22,000 men, women and children of Japanese origin driven from their west coast homes and imprisoned in detention centres for the duration of the war, many were also deported to Japan after the war. Three quarters of those evacuated and detained were born in Canada. To add insult to injury, they were required to pay for their internment. To do this they had to sell their homes, businesses, property and fishing boats at rock bottom prices.

No one can quarrel with the right of any nation to take extraordinary measures in time of war to guard against espionage and possible sabotage. The sudden and unprovoked attack on Pearl Harbour, December 7, 1941, by the Japanese Air Force, undoubtedly gave the Canadian Government some concern about the security of its western coastline, particularly when we remember that of the 23,000 Canadians of Japanese descent living in Canada, 22,000 resided in British Columbia. However, a closer examination reveals that the Canadian Government's policy was more a reaction to the anti-Oriental feeling which had pervaded British Columbian society for almost a century, rather than the possibility of Japanese-Canadian collaboration with the enemy.

Anti-Oriental feeling in Canada first began in British Columbia in 1858, the year that Crown colony was established. It was also the year of the Caribou Gold Rush, and the start of Chinese immigration to British Columbia to fill the need for cheap labour. In the 1880s, Japanese immigrants arrived on Canada's west coast and following the Chinese immigrant pattern, provided cheap labour for railway construction, mining and logging.

Although Canada was prepared to welcome Orientals as a source of cheap labour, it was not prepared to consider them as persons. Only a "person" was entitled to vote in federal elections and a person was so defined that Chinese and Mongolians were excluded. British Columbia went even further and passed legislation in 1895 denying the right to vote to all Orientals whether they were naturalized or Canadian born citizens.

Although the Parliament of Canada in 1898 gave naturalized Orientals the right to vote in federal elections, those rights could not be effectively exercised, because the federal government used the provincial voter's list to prepare their own list, and orientals were excluded from the provincial voter's list by provincial legislation. Even the courts could find nothing objectionable about these racist laws.

Orientals were also disqualified from participating in every aspect of public life. They were denied the right to employment by the provincial and municipal governments. A requirement that articled law students had to be on the voter's list effectively excluded them from becoming lawyers. Regulations were also passed by the federal government to restrict their involvement in the fishing industry on the west coast. Steps were also taken to restrict immigration of Orientals in the 1920s by Prime Minister Mackenzie King. However, there was one area in which they were not restricted — the armed forces. During the First World War, 202 Japanese Canadians enlisted and 59 of them died for their country.

On September 10, 1939, Canada declared war on Germany. Many Japanese-Canadians tried to enlist, and some were accepted, but the federal government announced on January 8, 1941 that they were exempted from military service. This was done to prevent any possible claim of a right to vote based on military service. Following the attack on Pearl Harbour, the Canadian Government moved quickly. All persons of Japanese descent, whether citizens or not, were required to register with the Registrar of Enemy Aliens. Although Canada had been at war with Germany and Italy since September 1939, no similar requirement was imposed on Canadian citizens of German and Italian origin.

Within two months, all persons of Japanese ancestry were ordered to be evacuated from the west coast and moved to detention and labour camps in the interior. All of their property was confiscated and sold. That order was enforced until 1944, long after it was clear that the prospect of a Japanese invasion of the west coast was highly remote.

What was the authority which gave the Canadian Government the right to single out the Japanese-Canadian for such unusual treatment? It was a statute passed over 25 years earlier in 1914 to deal with the emergency in Canada created by the Great War. Its long title was "An Act to confer certain powers upon the Governor in Council in the event of war, invasion or insurrection." Its short title was the War Measures Act. Its purpose was to give to the Canadian Government extraordinary and unlimited powers to pass regulations by order-in-council which had the effect of law without the necessity of obtaining the approval of Parliament. Section 2 of that Act provided:

> The issue of a proclamation by His Majesty, or under the authority of the Governor in Council shall be conclusive evidence that war, invasion, or insurrection, real or apprehended, exists and has existed for any period of time therein stated, and of its continuance, until by the issue of a further proclamation it is declared that the war, invasion or insurrection no longer exists.

Once a proclamation was issued, then section 3 of the Act came into effect:

> The Governor in Council may do and authorize such acts and things, and make from time to time such orders and regulations as he may by reason of the existence of real or apprehended war, invasion or insurrection deem necessary or advisable for the security, defence, peace, order and welfare of Canada; and for greater certainty, but not so as to restrict the generality of the foregoing terms, it is hereby declared that the powers of the Governor in Council extend to all matters coming within the classes of subjects hereinafter enumerated, namely. . . .

It gave to the Canadian Government extraordinary powers that few Canadians would tolerate in peacetime. The government, by simply passing an order-in-council, could censure, control and suppress any form of free speech or publication. By a simple order-in-council the government could arrest, detain or deport anyone suspected of being an alien enemy. That person had no recourse to the courts. A judge had no authority to decide if there was any basis for the suspicion or even enquire into whether there was any foundation for the government's action. The person who was arrested had no right to insist that he be brought to trial without the consent of the Minister of Justice. If the government wanted to keep him in custody indefinitely without trial, it could do so and he had no remedy. Furthermore, any of his property could be taken and forfeited or sold by the government.

After the hostilities with Germany ceased in 1919, the government did not repeal this statute. It remained as part of the law for another 20 years when it was invoked once again. On January 16, 1942 the Government of Canada passed an order-in-council authorizing the Minister of National Defence to declare certain parts of Canada as a "protected area." Once an area was declared a "protected area", the Minister of Justice had the power to require all enemy aliens to leave such protected area and to order their detention in any other area. On February 26, 1942, the Minister of Justice, Louis St. Laurent, issued an order requiring "every person of the Japanese race" to leave the protected area forthwith. This was followed by another order-in-council on March 4, 1942 regulating the evacuation of Japanese Canadians and authorizing a government custodian to confiscate and to sell their property.

By mid-1944, when it became evident that the Allied forces would soon win the war, the Canadian Government was faced with the problem of what to do with Japanese-Canadians in detention camps. They were not wanted by the Occidental population of British Columbia. Bowing to pressure, the Canadian Government gave them a choice between relocating east of the Rockies or being repatriated to Japan. To accomplish this, the government introduced a new bill into Parliament, the National Emergency Transitional Powers Act, which was approved by the Governor-General on December 18, 1945. That Act authorized the governor-in-council to continue to rule Canadians by way of regulations passed by orders-in-council.

Three orders-in-council were immediately passed ordering deported to Japan all Japanese nationals who had requested repatriation, or Canadian born or naturalized Canadians of Japanese origin who had requested repatriation but had not revoked that request in writing prior to September 1, 1945, the day before the unconditional surrender of Japan. Ten thousand Japanese Canadians had signed requests for repatriation. Three-quarters of these were Canadian citizens; one-half were Canadian born who knew no other country but Canada.

As the Canadian Government proceeded to act with indecent haste to deport Japanese Canadians, the fear of the oriental now gave way to a sense of shame. Across the country, Canadians began to protest the deportations. Prime Minister Mackenzie King, realizing that he had an unpopular situation on his hands, decided to refer the legality of the orders-in-council to the Supreme Court of Canada. The majority of the Court concluded that the government had exclusive authority to decide "the necessity or advisability of these measures" and that opinion was supported by the Judicial Committee of the Privy Council in England upon further appeal.

By this time, however, the voice of Canadians had become strong and persuasive. On January 24, 1947, the government decided to abandon its deportation programme. Unfortunately, for 4,000 Japanese Canadians, half of whom were born in Canada, it was too late. They had already been "repatriated" to a home that they had never really known. Japanese Canadians also had to wait another two years before they could return to the west coast. Finally on June 15, 1948 they were given the right to vote in federal elections. The right to vote in provincial elections in British Columbia was extended to them the following year.

## The October Crisis

Speaking at the opening of the Japanese Cultural Centre in Toronto on June 7, 1964, Prime Minister Lester B. Pearson reflected on the Japanese evacuation two decades earlier. He described "that action by the Canadian Government — though taken under the strains, and fears and pressure of war — ... a black mark against Canada's traditional fairness and devotion to principles of human rights." Canada he acknowledged "had no reason to be proud of this episode." But as we all know, it was a time of war. Although the action of the government could never be condoned, one could understand, in retrospect, why such steps had been taken to deny certain Canadian citizens their fundamental rights. Such arbitrary powers would never be exercised in peacetime by a government devoted to principles of fundamental freedom and justice.

On October 16, 1970, the Government of Canada issued the following proclamation:

Whereas the War Measures Act provides that the issuance of a proclamation under the authority of the Governor in Council shall be conclusive evidence that insurrection, real or apprehended, exists and has existed for any period of time therein stated and of its continuance, until by the issue of a further proclamation it is declared that the insurrection no longer exists.

And Whereas there is in contemporary Canadian society an element or group known as Le Front de Libération du Québec who advocate and resort to the use of force and the commission of criminal offences including murder, threat of murder and kidnapping as a means of or as an aid in accomplishing a governmental change within Canada and whose activities have given rise to a state of apprehended insurrection within the Province of Quebec.

Now Know Ye that We, by and with advice of Our Privy Council of Canada, do this by Our Proclamation proclaim and declare that apprehended insurrection exists and has existed as and from the sixteenth day of October, one thousand nine hundred and seventy.

What was the "apprehended insurrection" that had existed since the previous day that justified the Canadian Government in taking the unusual step of invoking the War Measures Act? Canada was certainly not at war with any country.

Shortly after nine o'clock on Monday October 5, 1970, four men rang the doorbell at the home of the British Trade Commissioner, James Cross, in Montreal. Under the pretext that they had a birthday present for him, Cross was abducted and kept captive for 51 days. The four men identified themselves as members of the liberation cell of the Front de Libération du Québec (F.L.Q.). They demanded the release of 23 "political prisoners" and $500,000 in gold bullion, as well as a number of other demands, otherwise Cross would be executed.

Understandably, neither the Canadian Government nor the Quebec Government were prepared to give in to these extortionate demands, although the federal government did agree to read the F.L.Q. Manifesto over the National Radio and Television Service. There were attempts made by the police to find Cross but they were all unsuccessful.

Five days later on Saturday October 10, 1970, Pierre Laporte, the Quebec Minister of Labour, was playing touch football with his nephew outside his home in Montreal when he was kidnapped by four men who identified themselves as members of the F.L.Q.'s Chenier cell.

Although some prominent members of the Quebec community such as Rene Levesque, leader of the Parti Québecois, and Claude Ryan, editor of *Le Devoir*, asked the government to compromise by releasing some of the prisoners, the Premier of Quebec, Robert Bourassa, was prepared to offer no more than safe passage out of Canada for the kidnappers of both Cross and Laporte, once they released their captives. When this offer was refused, Mr. Bourassa and Jean Drapeau, Mayor of Montreal, wrote letters to the Prime Minister in the early hours of Friday, October 16, asking the federal government to invoke emergency powers "to apprehend and keep in custody individuals who, the Attorney General of Quebec has valid reasons to believe, are determined to overthrow the government through violence and illegal means." In the words of Premier Bourassa, "we are facing a concerted effort to intimidate and overthrow the government and the democratic institutions of this province through planned and systematic illegal action, including insurrection."

Acting upon this request, the federal government issued the proclamation and passed an order-in-council declaring the F.L.Q. an unlawful association and making it a crime punishable with five years' imprisonment to be a member. The regulations also gave the police authority to arrest without warrant anyone whom they suspected was a member of the F.L.Q., as well as the right to enter any premises without warrant to carry out a search and seizure, if they had reason to suspect that the person was a member of the F.L.Q. There was no necessity for the police to act only on reasonable and probable grounds as the common law has required for centuries. Nor was anyone who was arrested entitled to be released on bail unless the Attorney General of the province consented. However, if after ninety days, his trial date was not set, he could apply to a judge of the Superior Court to fix a date for his trial.

In 1960, the Parliament of Canada had enacted the Bill of Rights which declared that no act of Parliament shall be so construed and applied so as to "authorize . . . the arbitrary detention, imprisonment or exile of any person . . . , deprive a person who has been arrested or detained of the remedy by way of *habeas corpus* for the determination of the validity of his detention and for his release if detention is not lawful . . ." and "deprive a person . . . of the right to reasonable bail without just cause." However, section 6 of the Canadian Bill of Rights also provided that any thing done or authorized under the War Measures Act was deemed not to be an "abrogation, abridgement or infringement of any right or freedom" recognized by the Canadian Bill of Rights.

Acting under these arbitrary emergency powers, the Quebec police force arrested almost 500 suspects and detained them in custody. Only 62 persons were charged with any crime under the regulation and less than 12 were convicted and sentenced.

The day after the proclamation was issued, Pierre Laporte's body was found in the trunk of a motor vehicle. He had been strangled. On December 3, 1970, James Cross was released by his abductors when the Quebec Government agreed to provide them with safe passage out of Canada.

## Arbitrary Detention and The Charter

Section 9 of the Charter of Rights and Freedoms guarantees that "everyone has the right not to be arbitrarily detained or imprisoned." An arbitrary detention is one that is capricious, frivolous, unwarranted and contrary to normal standards. In other words there must be some factual basis upon which it can be said that the police officer has reasonable grounds to believe that the person he is arresting or detaining has committed a crime or is in possession of evidence of a crime. Parliament cannot pass laws which authorize a police officer to arrest or detain anyone based on suspicion alone. The standard yardstick to be used both by Parliament or the provincial legislatures and the police is one of reasonable and probable cause.

Nowhere in the Charter of Rights and Freedoms is there any exception from this standard authorizing the government to invoke the arbitrary powers of the War Measures Act in times of crisis or emergency. Section 1 of the Charter does recognize that our rights and freedoms are subject "only to such reasonable limits prescribed by law as can be demonstrably justified in a free and democratic society." But it is the government that must justify its derogation from the fundamental rights and freedoms that the Charter seeks to protect. More important, of course, is the fact that the courts are no longer impotent to intervene as they were during the war years and during the October crisis in Quebec. Section 52 of the Charter makes it clear that "The Constitution of Canada is the supreme law of Canada, and any law that is inconsistent with the provisions of the Constitution is, to the extent of the inconsistency, of no force or effect."

# 6

# Freedom From Unreasonable Search and Seizure

The poorest man may in his cottage bid defiance to all the forces of the Crown. It may be frail — its roof may shake — the wind may blow through it — the storm may enter — the rain may enter — but the King of England cannot enter — all his force dares not cross the threshold of the ruined tenement.

William Pitt, Earl of Chatham (1763)

Many historians have not been very kind to John Wilkes — and maybe they were justified. His record as a parliamentarian was insignificant in an age that produced William Pitt and Edmund Burke. He was by his own admission an insatiable and notorious libertine, although profligacy was common amongst the rich upper classes. His real legacy was his fight for freedom of the press and the right to be secure against arbitrary intrusion by the state.

John Wilkes was born in London in 1725 (or if one is to accept his own account in 1727), the second son of Israel Wilkes, a successful malt distiller. Although extremely ugly in appearance, characterized by sunken eyes and a horrible squint, he was a man of irrepressible wit who charmed almost anyone who fell under his spell. At the age of 22 he dutifully agreed to marry the daughter of an old family friend, Mary Meade, who was also the heiress to a sizeable fortune and the Manor Aylesbury in Buckinghamshire. Although the marriage was disastrous from the beginning, it provided him with a daughter to whom he was totally devoted and a comfortable fortune. This enabled him to assume the role of a country gentleman and provided him with an introduction to the leading politicians, actors, writers and men of business and fashion of the period.

A new acquaintance, Thomas Potter, the member of Parliament for Aylesbury, introduced him into the Congenial Society of the Medmanham Monks. This was a social club who met occasionally in the rooms of St. Mary's Abbey at Medmanham in Buckinghamshire to indulge in obscene orgies and to parody the Roman Catholic ritual. Other leading members were Sir Francis Dashwood and the Fourth Earl of Sandwich. This club was more infamously known as the Hellfire Club.

In 1757, he stood for election to Parliament for Aylesbury at the suggestion of Potter who had chosen another constituency. He was elected but not before bribing most of his constituents — a practice not uncommon in those days among the gentry who wished to obtain a seat in Parliament. He soon came under the influence and patronage of Lord Temple and William Pitt. King George II was on the throne of England, William Pitt was the Prime Minister and England was in the midst of the Seven Years War.

Three years later in 1760, George III ascended the English throne. The King, who wanted an end to the war, forced Pitt's resignation and appointed his tutor, Lord Bute, as the new first minister on May 29, 1762. Within days, John Wilkes launched a weekly political paper, called *The North Briton*, to attack the new administration under Lord Bute.

The attacks were successful. In April 1763, Bute resigned, citing reasons of ill health and lack of support from his own cabinet. However, George Grenville, the new first minister, decided that opponents of the government must be silenced. Wilkes, one of the most vocal critics, was high on the list. On April 23, 1763 issue No. 45 of *The North Briton* was published. It was a vitriolic attack on the King's speech from the throne. After carefully pointing out that it was really not the King's speech that was being criticised since ". . . it had always been considered by the legislature, and by the public at large, as the speech of the minister", the article went on,

> Every friend of his country must lament that a prince of so many great and amiable qualities . . . can . . . give the sanction of the sacred name to the most odious measures . . . this week has given to the public the most abandoned instance of ministerial effrontery ever attempted. . . . I wish as much as any man in England to see the honour of the Crown maintained in a manner truly becoming Royalty. . . . I lament to see it sunk even to prostitution.

Notwithstanding the respectful references to him, King George III was furious. But his ministers were not sure about how they should proceed. The Attorney General and the Solicitor General were asked for their opinion and they advised that No. 45 could be judged "an infamous and seditious libel, tending to inflame the minds, and alienate the affections of the people from His Majesty and to excite them to traitorous insurrections against his government."

Relying on this opinion, the Secretary of State, Lord Halifax decided that Wilkes should be charged with "treasonable libel." A general warrant was issued by him for the arrest of the writers, printers, and publishers of the newspaper and for the seizure of their papers.

The Criminal Code of Canada provides that before a warrant may be issued for the arrest of someone or to authorize the search of premises, someone must swear an information outlining the factual basis why the warrant should be issued and that information must be presented to a justice of the peace. If the justice of the peace is satisfied that the allegations set out in the information support the issuance of a warrant of arrest or a warrant to search premises, he may proceed to issue it. A justice of the peace is an independent judicial officer who must exercise his discretion free of any control by the government.

Prior to April 1763, no one had ever questioned the right of the Secretary of State to issue a general warrant authorizing the person named in the warrant to enter any premise and to arrest anyone suspected of publishing seditious material. That right had been exercised for over two centuries by the infamous Star Chamber whose duty it was to suppress any form of dissent against the Crown. The Star Chamber had passed a number of decrees to regulate the manner of printing and the number of presses which could operate. A person could only print if he had a licence issued by the Secretary of State. To enforce its regulations, the court had exercised an unrestricted right to issue general warrants to search premises and confiscate any form of publication, and to imprison anyone suspected of having published it. But the Star Chamber had been abolished in 1640, and the licensing acts had lapsed in 1694. Nevertheless, the Secretary of State continued to issue general warrants even though there was no law authorizing it.

At the same time that general warrants were being issued without restraint by the Secretary of State, the common law was at work developing its own protection against arbitrary search warrants. It was now becoming accepted that a justice of the peace could issue a warrant if he received an information upon oath from the prosecutor or a witness. The information had to state that a felony had been committed and outline the causes of the suspicion. The great judge and scholar, Sir Matthew Hale wrote that warrants were not to be granted unless the complainant had "probable cause" to suspect the allegedly stolen goods were "in such house or place" and showed the reasons for "such suspicion." In addition, Hale expressed the view that the warrant should specify the name or description of the person to be arrested. It could not have a blank space to be filled in with the name of the person after the arrest had taken place.

On April 26, 1763, Lord Halifax issued the general warrants, addressed to four messengers of the King, authorizing and requiring them "to make strict and diligent search for the authors, printer, and publishers of a seditious and treasonable paper, entitled The North Briton, Number XLV . . ." and to arrest and bring them before him. John Wilkes was not named nor was anyone else.

In three days, the four messengers and a constable who accompanied them arrested 48 persons — many of whom had nothing to do with *The North Briton* — and brought them before Lord Halifax. Included were the publisher and printer of other issues of *The North Briton*. Although Wilkes was suspected of being behind No. 45, messengers did not arrive at his premises until April 30. At their request he went with them to the home of

Lord Halifax where Lord Egremont was also present. Both accused him of publishing No. 45. When he refused to answer their questions, they ordered him sent to the Tower of London. In the meantime, the messengers ransacked his home and seized all of his papers.

Immediately, Wilkes's friends brought an application for *habeas corpus* before Lord Chief Justice Pratt of the Court of Common Pleas who ordered that Wilkes be produced before him. On May 6, the Chief Justice ordered his release. As a member of Parliament, Wilkes was entitled to the privilege to be free from arrest in all cases except treason, felony and actual breach of the peace. Seditious libel was none of these things.

A number of persons who had been arrested and had their papers seized, including Wilkes, immediately sued the messengers and Lord Halifax for damages for trespass. The Chief Justice ruled that the "general warrants were illegal" and the juries were asked to assess the damages. Awards were given ranging from £200 to £400. Wilkes's case was tried by the Chief Justice on December 6, 1763. He was awarded £1,000 damages by the jury. The verdict was appealed to the full Court of King's Bench but it was not successful. Lord Mansfield and the whole court gave a unanimous opinion that general warrants were illegal.

While these proceedings were taking place, another famous case was tried before the courts, *Entick v. Carrington.* John Entick was involved in publishing *The Monitor,* also a weekly paper that attacked the government of the day. On November 11, 1762, the King's messengers, armed with a general warrant, entered his home and searched for copies of his publication. Entick also sued the messengers and Lord Halifax for trespass and was awarded £300. Chief Justice Pratt decided that the matter should be referred to the full court for a final determination as to the legality of the general warrants. It was heard three years later.

On behalf of Lord Halifax it was argued that even though the licensing acts had lapsed in 1694, the right of a Secretary of State to issue a general warrant had never been questioned in over 65 years. However, the main argument advanced was that such power was necessary in the interests of good government and public order. To that argument, Pratt who was now Lord Camden, delivered his famous reply:

> ... and with respect to the argument from state necessity, or a distinction that has been aimed at between state offences and others, the common law does not understand that kind of reasoning, nor do our books take notice of such distinctions.

The obligation was upon those who claim the power and authority to enter a man's home and to search and seize his papers to establish that he had legal authority to do so. If it were otherwise, then, said Lord Camden, "the secret cabinets and bureaus of every subject in this kingdom will be thrown open to the search and inspection of a messenger, whenever the secretary of state shall think fit to charge, or even suspect, a person to be author, printer, or publisher of a seditious libel." He summed up the common law of England in these now memorable words:

> By the laws of England, every invasion of private property, be it ever so minute, is a trespass. No man can set his foot upon my ground without my licence, but he is liable to an action, though the damage be nothing; which is proved by every declaration in trespass, where the defendant is called upon to answer for bruising the grass and even treading upon the soil. If he admits the fact, he is bound to show by way of justification that some positive law has empowered or excused him. The justification is submitted to the judges, who are to look into the books; and see if such a justification can be maintained by the text of the statute law. If no such excuse can be found or produced, the silence of the books is an authority against the defendant, and the plaintiff must have judgment.

After *Entick v. Carrington* was decided, the question of general warrants was raised in the House of Commons. Now, not even the law officers of the Crown were prepared to argue in favour of their legality. At long last the House of Commons decided to condemn their use not only in cases of libel but their use generally.

## The Writs are Denounced in the Colonies

At the same time that the legality of general warrants was being questioned in England, the legality of another warrant was being questioned in America — the writ of assistance. This writ, which was not really a search warrant at all, had its genesis in an act passed in 1662 during the reign of Charles II. Entitled "An Act for Preventing Frauds, And Regulating Abuses in His Majesty's Customs", or more simply the Act of Frauds, it authorized customs officers to enter any premises during the day to search and seize for any goods or merchandise "prohibited and uncustomed."

The writ of assistance, like the general warrant, was not issued by an impartial judicial officer who had to be satisfied by information under oath that there were reasonable and probable grounds to believe that prohibited goods were in a particular premise. The writ was issued by a minister of the Crown in charge of enforcing the customs laws. The writ had to carry the seal of the Court of Exchequer but that was merely a matter of form. The Court of Exchequer could not control the customs officer who issued it. In fact, the writ of assistance, once issued, remained valid during the life of the sovereign in whose name it was issued and automatically expired six months after his death.

In the new colonies, a triangular trade route had developed between Africa, the West Indies and New England. The cargo — rum, molasses and slaves — was bringing new wealth to the colonial merchant and the Crown wanted its share of the tariffs. England was heavily in debt from its war with France. Tariffs, of course, could only be collected if smuggling could be suppressed. Armed with writs of assistance, royal customs officers carried out random and indiscriminate searches of homes and businesses for undeclared cargo in an effort to carry out the tariff laws.

While England was in the throes of the Seven Years War with France, there was little opposition in America to English customs officers using issued writs of assistance to combat war-time trade between France and some northern colonial merchants and ship owners. But after King George II's death in October 1760, opposition developed against the issuance of new writs. George III was only 22 and it was likely that these new writs would continue to run long after the war. An application was made to the Massachusetts Superior Court to renew the writs of assistance but 63 Boston merchants united to oppose the application. James Otis, Jr., and Oxenbridge Thacher, two well-known Boston lawyers, were retained by merchants to oppose the petition for renewal. In fact, Otis had resigned his post as Advocate General of Massachusetts Bay to be able to argue the case. Against them for the Crown was their old mentor, Jeremiah Gridley. The case was heard by Thomas Hutchinson, Chief Justice of Massachusetts, in the old Council Chamber of the Townhouse in February 1761.

Otis denounced the writs of assistance as "the worst instrument of arbitrary power, the most destructive of English liberty, and the fundamental principles of law, that ever was found in an English law book," because they placed "the liberty of every man in the hands of every petty officer." He argued that general warrants and writs of assistance were not known to the common law; the common law only recognized special warrants and then only in cases of "great public necessity," "upon process and oath" and after the showing of "grounds of suspicion." Notwithstanding the eloquence of the plea, Chief Justice Hutchinson reserved judgment in order to enquire from England if the Court of Exchequer there issued general writs. After receiving an affirmative reply, he finally decided in favour of the customs officers. A young lawyer watching the trial, John Adams, who was later to become the second President of the United States, made notes of the proceedings. He wrote,

> Then and there was the first scene of the first opposition to the arbitrary claims of Great Britain. Then and there the child Independence was born.

Between 1776 and 1787, almost every American state adopted some type of provision protecting its citizens from arbitrary search and seizure. Finally, on December 15, 1791, the first ten amendments to the Constitution of the United States were ratified by the state legislatures. The Fourth Amendment declared:

> The right of the people to be secure in their persons, houses, papers, and effects, against unreasonable searches and seizures, shall not be violated, and no Warrant shall issue but upon probable cause, supported by Oath or affirmation, and particularly describing the place to be searched, and the persons or things to be seized.

Almost 100 years later, Mr. Justice Bradley of the Supreme Court of the United States spoke of the judgment of Lord Camden in *Entick v. Carrington* as "one of the landmarks of English liberty . . ." and "one of the permanent monuments of the British Constitution." In *Boyd v. United States*, he considered,

> The principles laid down in this opinion affect the very essences of constitutional liberty and security. They reach farther than the concrete form of the case then before the court, with adventitious circumstances; they apply to all invasions on the part of the government and all its employees of the sanctity of a man's home and privacies of life. It is not the breaking of his doors, and the rummaging of his drawers, that constitutes the essence of the offence; but it is the invasion of his indefeasible right of personal security, personal liberty and private property, where that right has never been forfeited by his conviction of some public offence, — it is the invasion of this sacred right which underlies and constitutes the essence of Lord Camden's judgment. Breaking into a house and opening boxes and drawers are circumstances of aggravation; but any forcible and compulsory extortion of a man's own testimony or of his private papers to be used as evidence to convict him of a crime or to forfeit his goods, is within the condemnation of that judgment. In this regard the Fourth and Fifth Amendments run almost into each other.
>
> Can we doubt that when the Fourth and Fifth Amendments to the Constitution of the United States were penned and adopted, the language of Lord Camden was relied on as expressing the true doctrine on the subject of searches and seizures, and as furnishing the true criteria of the reasonable and "unreasonable" character of such seizures?

*Boyd v. United States* soon became regarded as the cornerstone of the American law of search and seizure. We see in the passage quoted from the judgment of Justice Bradley a recognition of the close relationship between the Fourth Amendment protection against unreasonable search and seizure and the Fifth Amendment protection against self incrimination. To assist the government in enforcing the customs revenue law, Congress had passed on June 22, 1874, a provision which authorized the court, in revenue cases, to require anyone accused of violating the law to produce in court his private books, invoices, and papers. If he failed to do so, it would amount to a confession that he had imported merchandise fraudulently. In the Boyd case, customs officials had seized 35 cases of plate glass, and the court had ordered the defendant to produce the invoice for the plate glass because it was alleged that it would prove a breach of the Revenue Act.

Mr. Justice Bradley held that an action which required compulsory production was invalid for two reasons. First, it authorized an unreasonable search and seizure. Secondly, it had the effect of telling the person to be a witness against himself or to furnish evidence of a possible crime.

## Development of the Fourth Amendment

When we examine the Fourth Amendment, we see that there are two requirements which must be established by government officials to the satisfaction of the court before a search can be conducted. The first is that the search must be "reasonable." Secondly, a warrant may not issue except upon "probable cause, supported by Oath or affirmation, and particularly describing the place to be searched, the persons or things to be seized." Can there be a search without a warrant? This is a problem which has engaged the Supreme Court of the United States over the last century. To date, the question has not been answered definitely.

Probably no case reflects the diverging judicial views as much as the Court's decision in *Harris v. United States*. In that case, Harris was suspected of forging a cheque and using the mails to defraud. Agents of the Federal Bureau of Investigation obtained a warrant for his arrest on a charge of violating the postal laws and the National Stolen Property Act and went to his apartment to arrest him. The common law has always recognized that a policeman may only search an arrested person as an incident to a lawful arrest. The reasons for this are twofold. The first is to ensure that he will not destroy any evidence on his person relating to the specific offence for which he has been arrested. The second is to locate any item which may assist the accused to escape from custody and prevent him from causing harm to the arresting officer. The common law also recognized that, in some instances, the right to search for these two purposes extended beyond the particular individual concerned; it could cover things within his immediate physical control.

In the Harris case, the police did not stop after searching him and the immediate vicinity. They handcuffed him to a chair in the livingroom of his apartment and then, for five hours, conducted a thorough search of all the rooms. They ransacked his closets and dresser drawers, stripped his bed and looked under the carpets. They were looking for two cheques which they believed Harris stole and used in his mail-fraud scheme. Eventually, they found a sealed envelope labelled "personal papers" in a dresser drawer. It contained some Selective Service classification cards and registration certificates which Harris had no right to possess. He was charged and convicted of unlawfully possessing these articles.

Chief Justice Vinson rationalized the seizure in this way:

> In keeping the draft cards in his custody, petitioner was guilty of a serious and continuing offense against the laws of the United States. A crime was thus being committed in the very presence of the agents conducting the search. Nothing in the decisions of this court gives support to the suggestion that under such circumstances the law enforcement officials must impotently stand aside and refrain from seizing contraband material. If entry upon the premises be valid, there is nothing in the Fourth Amendment which inhibits the seizure by law-enforcement agents of government property the possession of which is a crime, even though the officers are not aware that such property is on the premises when the search is initiated.

In an eloquent dissenting opinion, Mr. Justice Frankfurter noted that,

> To find authority for ransacking a home merely from authority for the arrest of a person is to give a novel and ominous rendering to a momentous chapter in the history of Anglo-American freedom. An Englishman's home, though a hovel, is his castle, precisely because the law secures freedom from fear of intrusion by the police except under the careful safeguarded authorization by a magistrate. To derive from the common law right to search the person as an incident of his arrest the right of indiscriminate search of all his belongings, is to disregard the fact that the constitution protects both unauthorized arrest and unauthorized search. Authority to arrest does not dispense with the requirement of authority to search.
>
> But even if the search was reasonable, it does not follow that the seizure was lawful. If the agents had obtained a warrant to look for the cancelled checks, they would not be entitled to seize other items discovered in the process. . . . The Court's decision achieves the novel and startling result of making the scope of search without warrant broader than an authorized search.

Mr. Justice Murphy, in another dissenting opinion, pointed out that,

> The decision of the Court in this case can have but one meaning so far as searches are concerned. It effectively takes away the protection of the Fourth Amendment against unreasonable searches from those who are placed under lawful arrest in their homes. . . . Under today's decision, a warrant of arrest for a particular crime authorizes an unlimited search of one's home from cellar to attic for evidence of "anything" that might come to light, whether bearing on the crime charged or any other crime. A search warrant is not only unnecessary; it is a hindrance.

Today the debate still rages on in the Supreme Court of the United States. Should the first clause of the Fourth Amendment be read separately from the warrant clause; is the existence of a warrant only one factor in determining the reasonableness of a search; or must the two be read together so that warrantless searches are reasonable *per se*, subject only to certain exceptions where it would be impracticable to obtain a warrant?

There are, no doubt, situations where it would be unreasonable to expect the police officer to obtain a warrant. Instances recognized by the Supreme Court of the United States are:

1. Where the police officers are hotly in pursuit of the accused.
2. Where there are exigent circumstances such as where the police have reasonable cause to believe that the evidence exists and the delay in obtaining a warrant would almost certainly result in the loss or destruction of the evidence. For this reason it has been accepted that blood may be removed from a person where there are reasonable grounds to believe that he was driving while intoxicated. Scrapings from under the fingernails of a person suspected of strangling his wife have also been permitted.

3. The court has also authorized a search of vehicles where it is not practicable to obtain a warrant because the vehicle can be quickly out of the reach of the jurisdiction of the police officer.
4. Another exception recognized is where the article seized is in the plain view of the arresting officer and it would be foolish to expect him to abandon his investigation to obtain a warrant to seize that item.
5. Other exceptions recognized have been instances involving border searches, seizure for questioning and road blocks.

## Search and Seizure Since the Charter

Section 8 of the Charter of Rights and Freedoms ensures that,

Everyone has the right to be secure against unreasonable search or seizure.

There is nothing in this section which says that a search must be conducted only under the authority of a warrant. Indeed, earlier Canadian decisions cautioned the courts to avoid the temptation of embracing American authorities without acknowledging and recognizing the difficulties that have developed there. Some such as Mr. Justice Zuber reminded us that the Charter did not "intend a transformation of our legal system or the paralysis of law enforcement . . ." otherise it would ". . . only trivialize and diminish respect for the Charter." Mr. Justice Scollin warned that,

The Constitution is the safeguard of the citizen against the fist of the State: not his nanny. The task of protecting a person from State oppression and abuse does not require fevered solicitude for the private interest of the individual at the expense of the public interest he shares with his neighbours. To arm the individual is not to disarm the community, and particularly in the critical battlefield of search and seizure, if the Charter is not to become an instrument lethal to fact and reason, it is important not to emulate the quixotic crusades under the banner of the fourth amendment in the United States which have often glorified a law less reasonable than the search it condemned.

The trend of decisions following the Charter's implementation supported the view that the validity of a search and seizure did not depend on the existence of a search warrant. As long as the officers acted reasonably, in the sense that they acted upon reasonable and probable cause, the courts did not require a warrant to be issued. Of course, it was up to the court to determine whether, viewed objectively, the officers had acted upon reasonable and probable cause in conducting the search. Indeed, some courts went so far as to suggest that issuance of a search warrant by a justice of the peace did not make the search valid if it turned out that the warrant was issued upon improper or insufficient evidence.

However, on May 16, 1984, just two years after the Charter was proclaimed, the Ontario Court of Appeal, in *Regina v. Rao*, had some second thoughts about warrantless searches. In that case, the question was whether section 10(1)(*a*) of the Narcotic Control Act, which authorizes a warrantless search of any place other than a dwelling house where a peace officer reasonably believes that there is a narcotic present, was constitutionally valid. Mr. Justice Martin, delivering the judgment of the Court, noted that section 8 of the Charter, unlike the Fourth Amendment to the United States Constitution, does not contain a warrant clause. Nevertheless it was stressed that whether a search was authorized by a warrant was an important and even in some cases, a critical factor in assessing the reasonableness of a search in a given case. The requirement of the warrant provides a safeguard against an intrusion at the discretion of a police officer. It was designed to ensure that the justification for an intrusion would be determined in advance by an impartial judge rather than left to the arbitrary discretion of a police officer. However, he was not prepared to go so far as to say that it was an essential foundation to every search because there would, undoubtedly, be instances where it would be impracticable to obtain one.

On September 17, 1984, the Supreme Court of Canada finally declared in *Hunter v. Southam Inc,* that in all instances, a warrantless search was now *prima facie* unreasonable under section 8 of the Charter. The Court, of course, recognized that there would be instances where a warrant was not required and this was where it was not feasible to obtain one. However, the onus was upon the person seeking to justify a warrantless search to establish that it was not feasible to obtain one in the circumstances of that case. Chief Justice Dickson rationalized the position of the Court this way:

> If the issue to be resolved in assessing the constitutionality of searches . . . were whether *in fact* the governmental interest in carrying out a given search outweighed that of the individual in resisting the governmental intrusion upon his privacy, then it would be appropriate to determine the balance of the competing interests *after* the search had been conducted. Such a *post facto* analysis would, however, be seriously at odds with the purpose of s. 8. That purpose is, as I have said, to protect individuals from unjustified State intrusions upon their privacy. That purpose requires a means of *preventing* unjustified searches before they happen, not simply of determining, after the fact, whether they ought to have occurred in the first place. This, in my view, can only be accomplished by a system of *prior* authorization, not one of subsequent validation.
>
> A requirement of prior authorization, usually in the form of a valid warrant, has been a consistent prerequisite for a valid search and seizure both at common law and under most statutes. Such a requirement puts the onus on the State to demonstrate the superiority of its interests to that of the individual. As such it accords with the apparent intention of the Charter to prefer, where feasible, the right of the individual to be free from State interference to the interests of the State in advancing its purposes through such interference.
>
> I recognize that it may not be reasonable in every instance to insist on prior authorization in order to validate governmental intrusions upon individuals' expectations of privacy. Nevertheless, where it is feasible to obtain prior authorization, I would hold that such authorization is a pre-condition for a valid search and seizure.

His philosophy in adopting that approach was summed up in these words:

Anglo-Canadian legal and political traditions point to a higher standard. The common law required evidence on oath which gave "strong reason to believe" that stolen goods were concealed in the place to be searched before a warrant would issue. Section 443 of the *Criminal Code* authorizes a warrant only where there has been information upon oath that there is "reasonable ground to believe" that there is evidence of an offence in the place to be searched. The American *Bill of Rights* provides that "no warrants shall issue but upon probable cause, supported by oath or affirmation. . .". The phrasing is slightly different but the standard in each of these formulations is identical. The State's interest in detecting and preventing crime begins to prevail over the individual's interest in being left alone at the point where credibly-based probability replaces suspicion. History has confirmed the appropriateness of this requirement as the threshold for subordinating the expectation of privacy to the needs of law enforcement. Where the State's interest is not simply law enforcement as, for instance, where State security is involved or where the individual's interest is not simply his expectation of privacy as, for instance, when the search threatens his bodily integrity, the relevant standard might well be a different one.

# 7

# The Right to Habeas Corpus

... that no freeman shall be taken or imprisoned, but by the lawful judgment of his equals, or by the law of the land. And many subsequent old statutes expressly direct, that no man shall be taken or imprisoned by suggestion or petition to the king or his council, unless it be by legal indictment, or the process of the common law. By the petition of right, 3 Car. I, it is enacted, that no freeman shall be imprisoned or detained without cause shewn, to which he may make answer according to law. By 16 Car. I. c. 10. if any person be restrained of his liberty by order or decree of any illegal court, or by command of the king's majesty in person, or by warrant of the council board, or of any of the privy council; he shall, upon demand of his council, have a writ of habeas corpus, to bring his body before the court of king's bench or common pleas; who shall determine whether the cause of his commitment be just, and thereupon do as justice shall appertain. And by 31 Car. II. c. 2. commonly called the habeas corpus act, the methods of obtaining this writ are so plainly pointed out and enforced, that, so long as this statute remains unimpeached, no subject of England can be long detained in prison, except in those cases in which the law requires and justifies such detainer. And, lest this act should be evaded by demanding unreasonable bail, or sureties for the prisoner's appearance, it is declared by 1 W. & M. st. 2, c. 2. that excessive bail ought not to be required.

Sir William Blackstone, Commentaries on
the Laws of England, Vol. 1 (1775)

## The Writ of Habeas Corpus

The institution of slavery is probably as old as man himself. It was introduced in the New World because the European conqueror found that his misuse of the native Indian population as labour brought him into conflict with the missionaries whose main preoccupation was the conversion of the pagan population to Christianity. In 1517, Bartolome de Las Casas, Roman Catholic Bishop of Chiapas proposed a solution to Emperor Charles V of Germany. He suggested that each Spanish settler should be permitted to bring over a certain number of Negro slaves from Africa. This proposal was accepted. In due course, Spanish noblemen were granted letters patent to import a specified number of Africans into Hispaniola each year on condition of paying duties to the royal treasury.

Soon other European countries instituted the slave route to colonize the New World which they had just conquered. It is believed that between 1680 and 1786, 2,000,000 African slaves were brought to the British possessions and West Indies alone. But by the latter half of the 17th century, the anti-slavery movement had gained momentum. First hand reports, novels and plays describing the inhuman treatment inflicted upon slaves began to have an impact on British public opinion.

The problem reached its peak in the early part of the 18th century as planters brought their slave servants to England. What was the status of the slave? England at the time did not recognize slavery on English soil. Slavery, however, was accepted and continued to flourish in its colonies. In 1729, the matter was referred to the Attorney General and Solicitor General, who delivered their opinion pronouncing themselves in favour of the doctrine that a master could compel a slave to return to the colony, a view which conflicted with that of Chief Justice Sir John Holt. Finally, in 1772, the issue was settled by the famous decision of Lord Mansfield in the case of James Sommersett.

Sommersett, a Negro slave, had been purchased by Charles Steuart in America on October 1, 1769. Steuart set sail for England to transact some business and arrived in London November 10. Sommersett accompanied Steuart on the voyage as his servant. Two years later on October 1, 1771, Sommersett escaped, encouraged by members of the anti-slavery movement who offered him their assistance. But 57 days later he was captured by persons employed by Steuart and forcibly carried on board a ship, the Ann and Mary under the command of John Knowles. At the time, the ship was docked in the Thames River and was bound for Jamaica.

Thomas Walklin, Elizabeth Cade and John Marlow, all active in the anti-slavery movement, decided to test the confinement of Sommersett by Knowles while he was within the territorial jurisdiction of Great Britain. On December 3, 1771, they applied for a writ of *habeas corpus.*

A writ of *habeas corpus,* which means that you have the body, is a writ so called because it is directed to a person who detains another in custody. It commands him to produce or have the body of that person brought before the court so that the court can consider the legality of the detention. The writ, itself, was initially used to test the legality of imprisonment for political reasons, especially during the reigns of the Stuarts. It also became a method of scrutinizing the abuses of judges who, at the request of the Crown, detained state prisoners in prison. The result was the enactment of the Habeas Corpus Act in 1679. This Act, in effect, made the granting of *habeas corpus* compulsory in the case of a person imprisoned without a legal cause being assigned in the warrant of committal. It also provided for the speedy trial of persons imprisoned for treason or felony.

On December 9, 1771, John Knowles produced the body of James Sommersett before Lord Mansfield. He explained that his owner, Charles

Steuart had delivered an order into his hands to transport Sommersett to Jamaica to sell him as a slave. Affidavit material filed before the court established that Steuart had purchased Sommersett as a slave in Virginia and that he had brought him to England as his servant; but Sommersett had refused to return with him to Virginia.

On February 7, 1772, the case was argued before Lord Mansfield, who was Chief Justice of the King's Bench. Born in 1705, the son of the fifth Viscount Stormont he was Chief Justice of the King's Bench for 33 years. His fame as one of the Chief Justices of England was rivalled only by Sir Edward Coke and Sir Matthew Hale. Although his reputation and real influence on Anglo-American law was in the field of commercial law, his judgment in the Sommersett case was echoed in America until the "detestable commerce" of slavery was finally abolished.

Serjeant Davy who appeared as one of the counsel for Sommersett argued passionately on his behalf:

> To punish not even a criminal for offences against the laws of another country; to set free a galley-slave, who is a slave by his crime; and make a slave of a negro, who is one, by his complexion; is a cruelty and absurdity that I trust will never take place here: such as, if promulged, would make England a disgrace to all the nations under heaven: for the reducing a man, guiltless of any offence against the laws, to the condition of slavery, the worst and most abject state.

The final words of his argument have been repeated frequently over the centuries:

> However, it has been asserted, and is now repeated by me, this air is too pure for a slave to breathe in: I trust, I shall not quit this court without certain conviction of the truth of that assertion.

Lord Mansfield delivered his judgment on June 22, 1772. He spoke these memorable words:

> The state of slavery is of such a nature, that it is incapable of being introduced on any reasons, moral or political, but only by positive law, which preserves its force long after the reasons, occasion, and time itself from whence it was created, is erased from memory. It is so odious, that nothing can be suffered to support it, but positive law. Whatever inconveniences, therefore, may follow from the decision, I cannot say this case is allowed or approved by the law of England; and therefore the black must be discharged.

## Development of the Writ

It is believed that the first writ of *habeas corpus* was issued before the signing of the Magna Carta of 1215. Initially, it was used by officers of the Crown to bring cases from inferior courts into the King's courts as a means of extending the royal authority. It was not until the reign of Henry VII, 1485-1509, that it began to be used as a protection for persons imprisoned by the Privy Council. But at the beginning of the 17th century, judges, who were still subject to dismissal by the King, often frustrated attempts to have persons released by finding procedural defects in the writ of *habeas corpus*. In Darnel's Case, 1627, the courts went so far as to decide that the writ of *habeas corpus* could not release a person who was detained by the command of the King. In 1628, Parliament passed the Petition of Right in an effort to remedy this situation. In 1641, the statute which abolished the odious Court of Star Chamber also provided that anyone imprisoned by a court, the King, or the Privy Council should have the right of *habeas corpus* to test the legality of the committal. Finally in 1679, the Habeas Corpus Act was passed. It required judges to issue the writ when the court was adjourned for vacation. It also imposed severe penalties on any judge or officer of the Crown who refused to comply with it.

English settlers who came to North America brought the English common law with them. *Habeas corpus* as part of that common law heritage was adopted by many of the colonial courts. As early as 1692, Massachusetts and South Carolina passed legislation similar to the English Habeas Corpus Act of 1679. In fact, the right to *habeas corpus* was popularly regarded as one of the basic protections of individual liberty at the time of the outbreak of the American revolution. As recognition of its importance, it was enshrined in Article 1, Section 9, Paragraph 2, of the Constitution of the United States of America by representatives of the thirteen states meeting in Congress on July 4, 1776:

> The Privilege of the Writ of Habeas Corpus shall not be suspended, unless when in Cases of Rebellion or Invasion the public Safety may require it.

That first Congress also passed laws giving justices of the Supreme Court of the United States and judges of the District Court, the power to issue writs of *habeas corpus*.

## Habeas Corpus in Canada

English settlers in Canada also brought English common law with them. As each province was formed with its own legislature, British common law was proclaimed as the law of that province. *Habeas corpus* was first introduced into Quebec by the Royal Proclamation of 1763 and the Quebec Act of 1774. In 1784, the common law writ of *habeas corpus*, together with all of the changes made by the English Habeas Corpus Act of 1679, was proclaimed by the Ordinance of Governor Haldimand. In 1866 the province of Canada passed a statute called "An Act for More effectually Securing the Liberty of the Subject", authorizing wide use of *habeas corpus* in criminal proceedings. That statute became part of the law of Ontario when it joined the Confederation in 1867.

The Charter of Rights and Freedoms has entrenched this ancient remedy as a guarantee to all who may arbitrarily be imprisoned by the state. Section 10(*c*) provides:

10. Everyone has the right on arrest or detention,

(*c*) to have the validity of the detention determined by way of habeas corpus and to be released if the detention is not lawful.

# 8

# The Right to Remain Silent

You sit to answer one limited question. Has the prosecution satisfied you beyond reasonable doubt that Dr. Adams murdered Mrs. Morrell? On that question he stands upon his rights and does not speak. I have made it quite clear — have I not? — that I am not criticizing that. I do not criticize it at all. I hope that the day will never come when that right is denied to any Englishman. It is not a refuge of technicality, members of the jury. The law on this matter reflects the natural thought of England. So great is, and always has been our horror at the idea that a man might be questioned, forced to speak and perhaps to condemn himself out of his own mouth that we grant to everyone suspected or accused of crime at the beginning, at every stage and until the very end to say: "Ask me no questions. I shall answer none. Prove your case."

Charge to the jury by Lord Devlin in
*Regina v. John Bodkin Adams* (1957)

I would like to venture the suggestion that the privilege against self-incrimination is one of the greatest landmarks in man's struggle to make himself civilized. As I have already pointed out, the establishment of the privilege is closely linked historically with the abolition of torture. But torture was once used by honest and conscientious public servants as a means of obtaining information about crimes which would not otherwise be disclosed. We want none of that today, I am sure. For a very similar reason we do not make even the most hardened criminal sign his own death warrant, or dig his own grave, or pull a lever which springs the trap on which he stands. We have through the course of history developed a considerable feeling for the dignity and intrinsic importance of the individual man. Even the evil man is a human being.

Dean Erwin Griswold, The Fifth Amendment To-day (1955)

In 1637, John Lilburne was summoned to appear before the Attorney General's chief clerk to answer questions about his involvement in shipping seditious books into England from Holland. Lilburne was just 23 years of age. The second son of an old and respected family, John Lilburne was born and raised in the family manor, Thickly Punchardon, located about 350 miles north of London. His family, once prosperous, had suffered financially because of plagues and scanty harvests.

As the second son, John Lilburne could expect to receive little more than a cursory education in Latin and Greek. He had, however, also acquired a strong Puritan training from his family. This training bred in him a deep hatred for oppression and a great concern for the poor and disadvantaged.

At the age of 15, his father sent him to London to be apprenticed to a clothier. There he could be expected to earn his fortune. But the London that Lilburne found was not only one of the largest and richest cities in the world, it was also a hotbed of Puritanism.

On one occasion, he accompanied his master, also a Puritan, on a visit to prison to see Dr. John Bastwick. Bastwick, a physician, had been imprisoned in June 1637 along with Henry Burton, a preacher, and William Prynne, a lawyer, for having published a text about the Anglican bishops. Henry VIII had passed a statute in 1538 prohibiting the publication of any document without Royal approval. In 1637, Charles I was on the English throne. He had entrusted William Laud, the Archbishop of Canterbury, as the sole authority to issue licences to publish. Because it was hardly likely that Archbishop Laud would authorize a Puritan to publish pamphlets attacking the Anglican Church, the pamphlets were published in secret and distributed.

Eventually, these pamphlets came to the attention of the authorities. Bastwick, Burton and Prynne were arrested and convicted by the Court of High Commission for sedition. Each was fined £5,000 and sentenced to life imprisonment. But the Court of Star Chamber did not consider that this was sufficient punishment. It also sentenced the three men to mutilation by hacking off their ears, and to the pillory.

John Lilburne was present in the crowd gathered to witness the sentences being carried out. He was deeply moved by the martyrdom of these Puritan leaders. There soon developed a close friendship with Dr. Bastwick who took a personal interest in Lilburne's religious development.

While in prison, Dr. Bastwick had written another pamphlet attacking the bishops. Lilburne offered to smuggle it to Holland where it could be printed and smuggled back into England. Bastwick reluctantly agreed and Lilburne proceeded to undertake the task with the assistance of two other men. It was not long before thousands of the pamphlets were being distributed in England. Archbishop Laud, however, had planted informers among the Puritans. The two men who had assisted Lilburne in smuggling the pamphlets confessed to the authorities to save their own lives. In December 1637, less than six months after Lilburne had witnessed the public mutilations of Bastwick, Burton and Prynne, he found himself in prison. The Privy Council turned the case over to John Banks, the Attorney General for prosecution.

Today we accept as a basic underlying principle of our judicial system that no person is bound to accuse or incriminate himself. In the United

States, this right is specifically guaranteed by the Fifth Amendment to the Constitution. It provides that "no person . . . shall be compelled in any criminal case to be a witness against himself. . . ." A similar protection exists in England today under the common law. The Canadian Charter of Rights and Freedoms also specifically guarantees that protection in section 11(*c*) and section 13. In 1637, no such right existed in England.

In fact, a practice had developed almost 400 years earlier in the Ecclesiastical Court requiring a person to answer questions on oath about his involvement in matters the church considered to be heresy. It was known as the *ex officio* oath. In 1215, the same year as the Magna Carta was signed by King John at Runnymede, Pope Innocent III convened the Fourth Lateran Council. His aim was to ferret out and punish anyone guilty of an offence against Catholic orthodoxy. He introduced a new code of criminal procedure at the council. It was based upon the practice of Imperial Rome known as the "Inquisitio" or Inquiry.

The practice was simply this. Any judge could order the arrest of someone suspected of heresy or some other crime. The prisoner would be brought before the judge and ordered to take an oath to tell the truth to all the questions that might be put to him. He was not told of the specific crime that he was said to have committed or the names of the witnesses against him. This placed him in an intolerable position. If he told the truth, he might find that his answers could amount to a confession of a crime that he was not aware he had committed. If he lied, then he ran the risk of being charged with perjury.

If he refused to avoid both situations by saying nothing, he was usually thrown into a solitary cell for days, weeks, months and even years and kept just barely alive on a diet of foul water and stale bread. Physical torture, using the rack and screw, was eventually approved by Pope Innocent IV in 1252.

The "Inquisitio" or inquisitorial system of criminal procedure was unknown in 13th century England. The English common law was based on the accusatorial system. That system required an accusor to do so openly. The accusation had to be in writing and the accused was entitled to be tried by his neighbours and confronted in open court by the witnesses against him.

However, after the Norman conquest, William the Conqueror set up special Ecclesiastical Courts to hear cases involving the clergy. These courts, presided over by senior officials of the church, adopted the inquisitorial system which had developed in continental Europe.

Over the next two centuries, the Ecclesiastical Courts rose in prominence as they began to extend their jurisdiction beyond the clergy to the common Englishman in an effort to suppress heresy. Although there was an outcry by the common law courts and attempts by Parliament to restrain the Ecclesiastical Courts, they continued to grow. By the 15th century, warring factions of the nobility eventually resulted in Tudor monarchs achieving strong personal power. It was during this period that various courts developed out of the King's Privy Council. The Star Chamber, named for the golden stars which decorated the ceiling of the room, was formalized by an Act of Parliament in 1487. The other was the Court of High Commission whose role was to punish ecclesiastical offenders after Henry VIII became spiritual head of the Church of England. Both of these courts sought to destroy Lilburne for assisting Dr. Bastwick in spreading sedition. Both courts would find their own death warrants signed and sealed within five years.

Although Lilburne had received limited formal education, he understood his rights as an Englishman. Indeed, because he constantly challenged authority and insisted that he be granted the rights of every freeborn Englishman, he became known as "Freeborn John." To use his own words, he was "an honest true-bred freeborn Englishman that never in his life loved a tyrant or feared an oppressor."

After Lilburne was ordered by the Privy Council to be taken before the Attorney General, John Banks, he was taken to the Attorney General's Chambers. As Lilburne recounts the events, he "was referred to be examined by Mr. Cockshey, his chief clerk; and at our first meeting together he did kindly entreat me, and made me sit down by him, put on my hat, and began with me after this manner. Mr. Lilburne — what is your Christian name?"

As Lilburne reports, a number of questions were put to him gradually leading up to the matter which was apparently in issue. Lilburne answered many of the questions but at last refused to go any further. He told Cockshey, "I know it is warrantable by the law of God, and I think by the law of the land, that I may stand on my just defence, and not face your interrogatories, that my accusers ought to be brought face to face, to justify what they accuse me of." Lilburne refused to answer any more questions until his accusers were brought before him to accuse him face to face. He told the clerk that he would say nothing except that "he would answer no impertinent questions, for fear that with my answer I may do myself hurt."

At this stage, the clerk told Lilburne of what was contained in the sworn affidavit against him and Lilburne dismissed them as lies. He was told by the clerk that he could be forced to answer the questions but this apparently did not have any effect on him. Although he admitted that he had been to Holland and was aware of the existence of certain pamphlets, he refused to answer any more questions. "I am not willing to answer you to any more of these questions, because I see you go about this examination to ensnare me: for seeing the things for which I am imprisoned cannot be proved against me, you will get other matter out of my examination."

The clerk then brought Lilburne before the Attorney General who asked him to sign the statement which had been taken down by the clerk;

but he refused to do so. Lilburne requested, but was refused, the right to write down an answer of his own as to what was alleged against him. Because of his refusal to cooperate, Lilburne was returned to prison. There he remained for another two weeks until he was brought before the Court of Star Chamber to be examined *ex officio* upon oath. Again he refused to take the oath because he had not been provided with a statement of the charges against him. To the request by the clerk to take the Bible and swear, he replied:

> "to what?
> THE CLERK: That shall true answer to all things asked of you.
> LILBURNE: Must I do sir? But before I swear, I will know to what I must swear.
> THE CLERK: As soon as you have sworn, you shall but not before.

Lilburne persisted in refusing to take the oath until he was provided with a copy of the charge against him. The court was shocked. Although many had refused to take the oath when they had been brought up on religious charges, no one had ever challenged the authority of the Star Chamber to require the oath. However, as far as Lilburne was concerned, the two oaths were the same and he would not budge.

Lilburne remained in prison another six weeks. Once more, he was brought before the Star Chamber but again refused to take the oath. This time he was placed in solitary confinement. Another week passed and he was returned once more to the Star Chamber but again refused to take the oath. The Lords of the Star Chamber could no longer tolerate his insolence. He was fined £500 and ordered to be imprisoned indefinitely until he took the oath. He was also sentenced to be whipped from The Fleet to the pillory, a distance of two miles. As Lilburne described it, "I was condemned because I would not accuse myself."

When he arrived at the pillory, a messenger sent from the Star Chamber offered to spare him the pillory if he would take the oath. He refused. Courageously, he continued to speak to the crowd. After a half hour, the authorities could stand it no longer. A gag was stuffed in his mouth with such force that his mouth bled and he was left bare headed in the sun for two hours. For his insolence he was condemned by the Star Chamber to additional punishment. His legs and arms were shackled with double irons and he was thrown in the worst part of the prison. For ten days he was given no food and would have died if the other prisoners had not smuggled food to him. After four months in prison, he was eventually released from solitary confinement.

However, his ordeal was not over. He remained in prison for the next two and one half years. Throughout that period, he continued to write pamphlets about his trial and these were smuggled out to the public. His ordeal became an example for others who were similarly condemned, as they too began to refuse to take the oath.

King Charles dissolved Parliament in 1629 and ruled arbitrarily for eleven years. By 1640, he found himself in serious financial trouble. He needed the assistance of Parliament to provide him with funds and so agreed that it should reconvene. In November 1640, Parliament finally met after eleven years. By this time, it was dominated by Puritans who had acquired their wealth in commerce. Oliver Cromwell, making his first speech in Parliament, took up the cause of John Lilburne. Within a few days, Freeborn John as well as Bastwick, Prynne, Burton and others were released. More than three years after his arrest, Parliament resolved that "the sentence of the Star Chamber against John Lilburne is illegal, and against the liberty of the subject: and also bloody, cruel, barbarous and tyrannical." He was given compensation of £3,000.

On July 5, 1641, Parliament finally abolished the Courts of High Commission and the Star Chamber. It was ordered that no church authority could administer any oath where the answers might subject one "to any censure, pain, penalty or punishment whatsoever. . . . ."

## Trial by Jury in the Seventeenth Century

When John Lilburne refused to be examined *ex officio* upon oath before the Star Chamber, what he was really complaining about was that he was expected to answer questions when he had never been charged with any offence. It would never have crossed his mind to object to answering questions about a specific accusation. It was only the Ecclesiastical Courts which demanded the *ex officio* oath and subjected suspects to questioning. Common law courts could only act upon a specific accusation made in writing and approved by the grand jury. A person tried in those courts knew the exact charge made against him before his trial began.

However, trials, even in the common law courts, bore little resemblance to the system of trial by jury or by judge alone that we know today. Persons accused of a crime in the 17th century were not entitled to be represented by counsel. Nor were they entitled to call evidence in their defence. Standing alone in the prisoner's dock, they were expected to conduct their own defence by cross-examining the various witnesses that were called by the Crown. Generally, after these witnesses were called, the presiding judge or the lawyers representing the Crown would challenge the prisoner to confess his guilt or give some explanation of the evidence against him.

But the objection that "no man should be required to incriminate himself" (expressed in the Latin maxim — *nemo tenetur prodere se ipsum or nemo tenetur prodere accusare*) that had been raised in the Ecclesiastical Courts was now heard in the common law courts. By the end of the 17th century, it became a firmly established rule in all courts.

## Taking the Fifth in America

The thirteen states in America which were to make their famous Declaration on July 4, 1776 believed that the right to remain silent was so fundamental to their liberty that it had to be enshrined in their Bill of Rights. The Fifth Amendment passed by Congress on September 25, 1789 provided that,

> nor shall (any person) be compelled in any criminal case to be a witness against himself. . . .

But it was not until the second half of the 20th century that the right not to be "compelled in any criminal case to be a witness against himself" began to take on a new meaning. Now not only was a man entitled to refuse to answer any questions in a court proceeding that might tend to incriminate him, he was entitled to insist that he not be questioned by the police outside of court unless he freely and voluntarily agreed to be questioned. Furthermore, if he wished, he was entitled to have his lawyer present with him to advise on what questions to answer and what questions not to answer. Eventually, in 1964 the Supreme Court of the United States in the *Escobedo v. Illinois* case decided that not only was a person suspected of a crime entitled to have a lawyer present with him when he was questioned by the police, the police had a duty to tell him about his right to a lawyer. Two years later the Supreme Court of the United States went even further in the case of *Miranda v. Arizona*. Now there was not only an obligation upon the police to tell an accused about his right to have a lawyer present with him while he was being questioned, the police had to provide him with a lawyer if he was unable to afford one. It was only when a confession was made freely and voluntarily under all of these conditions, that it could be admitted in court against the accused.

## The Canadian Rule

Canadian courts have also recognized that a confession cannot be admitted unless it is free and voluntary. But until the Charter of Rights, the courts never said that an accused was entitled to have his lawyer present while he was being questioned by the police. Nor did the courts recognize that there was any obligation upon the police to tell the accused that he was entitled to have a lawyer present while they were questioning him or to provide him with counsel if he could not afford to hire one. However, if he asked to see his lawyer and that right was refused, a judge usually refused to admit a confession because there was a good chance that it was not given voluntarily.

Once an accused stepped into a witness box and gave testimony in any proceeding, he was considered to be a witness like any other witness.

Although the protection afforded by the American Fifth Amendment has always permitted a witness, whether an accused or otherwise, to refuse to answer a question that might tend to incriminate him, that has not been the case in Canada. In Canada, any person, even an accused, who steps into the witness box must answer any question put to him even if it tends to incriminate him. However, the Canada Evidence Act intervenes to prevent his testimony from being used against him in any other proceeding except a prosecution for perjury.

The Charter of Rights adds no further protections to those which have existed since the time of John Lilburne. Section 11(c) provides that,

> Any person charged with an offence has the right
>
> > (c)  not to be compelled to be a witness in proceedings against that person in respect of the offence.

Nor does section 13 of the Charter add any further protection than that already existing under the Canada Evidence Act. It still requires anyone who steps into the witness box to answer all questions that are put to him by counsel or the judge. It merely ensures that any answers given by him cannot be used against him in any other proceeding, except one for the giving of false evidence.

> 13.  A witness who testifies in any proceedings has the right not to have any incriminating evidence so given used to incriminate that witness in any other proceedings, except in a prosecution for perjury or for the giving of contradictory evidence.

There are many misconceptions by the public about the right to remain silent. It is clear under Canadian law that it means nothing more than that a person is not compelled to incriminate himself "out of his own mouth." It does not mean that he is entitled to demand that he not incriminate himself in other ways. For example, the Criminal Code of Canada requires a motorist to provide a sample of his breath to be analyzed in a breathalyzer machine when a police officer has reasonable and probable grounds to believe that the motorist is impaired or has consumed a quantity of alcohol so that the quantity in his blood exceeds 80 milligrams of alcohol in 100 millilitres of blood. The results of that breathalyzer test may then be used as evidence and be admissible against a motorist on a charge of impaired driving or driving with an alcohol level exceeding 80 milligrams of alcohol in 100 millilitres of blood. The argument that the compulsion of a breath sample infringes the motorist's right to remain silent has been firmly rejected by Canadian courts. Taking a blood sample from an unconscious motorist for analysis and the results of that test have also been considered by Canadian courts not to conflict with the motorist's right to remain silent.

What happens if an accused is asked to participate in a police identification line-up and he refuses to do so because he believes that he may be identified by the victim? If he refuses to do so, can the fact that he refused be evidence against him at his trial? Does it infringe his right to remain silent as guaranteed by section 11(c) of the Charter? The answer to that question undoubtedly lies in a decision given by the Supreme Court of Canada in 1973 in *Regina v. Marcoux and Solomon*. Mr. Justice Dickson who gave the judgment of the Court clearly stated what the privilege (the right to remain silent) means in Canadian law:

> The limit of the privilege against self-incrimination is clear. The privilege is the privilege of a witness not to answer a question which may incriminate him. That is all that is meant by the Latin maxim, *nemo tenetur se ipsum accusare*, often incorrectly advanced in support of a much broader proposition. . . .
>
> In short, the privilege extends to the accused quai witness and not quai accused; it is concerned with testimonial compulsion specifically and not with compulsion generally.

## Critics of Silence

There is probably no legal principle that arouses as much passion or is as misunderstood as the right to remain silent. One of its earliest and most vocal critics was the famous legal scholar, Jeremy Bentham. Writing in the early 1800s, he called the rule,

> One of the most pernicious and irrational rules that ever found its way into the human mind. . . . If all criminals of every class had assembled and framed a system after their own wishes, is not this rule the very first they would have established for their security? Innocence never takes advantage of it; innocence claims the right of speaking as guilt invokes the privilege of silence.

An equally bitter critic has been Mr. Justice Edson Haines of the Ontario Supreme Court. In 1972, he wrote,

> I submit that the greatest obstacle to efficient criminal law enforcement in Anglo-American jurisdictions is the right of the accused to remain silent. It is a luxury society can no longer afford. It contributes to the high success ratio of crime. It frustrates the police, comforts criminals, and encourages disrespect for the law. And with great deference to the legal profession, the abolition of the right to remain silent is necessary to save an honourable profession from its own dishonour.

Is the right to remain silent an obstacle to effective police investigation? Does it frustrate the police, comfort criminals and encourage a disrespect for the law? There are some who argue that compelling a person to incriminate himself would aid scientific methods of investigation. Others argue that it would only hinder. For example, a century ago, a famous criminal law judge Sir James Fitzjames Stephen, although in favour of abolishing the privilege recalled,

During the discussion which took place on the Indian Code of Criminal Procedure in 1872 some observations were made of the reasons which occasionally led native police officers to apply torture to prisoners. An experienced civil officer observed, "There is a great deal of laziness in it. It is far pleasanter to sit comfortably in the shade rubbing red pepper into a poor devil's eyes than to go about in the sun hunting up evidence." This was a new view to me, but I have no doubt of its truth.

The arguments that the right to remain silent hinders or promotes effective police investigation really fails to address the fundamental issue as to why the rule continues to exist. It does so because we, descendants of the common law tradition, recognize that in a free society the dignity of the individual is a higher right than the absolute security of society. This was stressed by the late Chief Justice Warren in his now celebrated judgment in *Miranda v. Arizona*. There he described the rule as "one which groped for the proper scope of government power over a citizen." He went on,

> The constitutional foundation underlying the privilege is the respect a government — state or federal — must accord to the dignity or integrity of its citizens. To maintain a "fair state-individual balance", to require the government "to shoulder the entire load", ... to respect the inviolability of the human personality, our accusatory system of criminal justice demands that government seeking to punish an individual produce the evidence against him by its own independent labors, rather than by cruel, simple expedient of compelling it from his own mouth . . . the privilege is fulfilled only when the person is guaranteed the right "to remain silent unless he chooses to speak in the unfettered exercise of his own will."

But the most compelling support for the privilege was given by Abe Fortas before he became a justice of the Supreme Court of the United States:

> The fundamental value that the privilege reflects is intangible, it is true; but so is liberty, and so is man's immortal soul. A man may be punished, even put to death by the state; but if he is an American or an Englishman or a free man anywhere, he should not be made to prostrate himself before its Majesty. Mea culpa belongs to man and his God. It is a plea which cannot be extracted from a free man by human authority. To require it is to insist that the State is the superior of the individuals who compose it, instead of their instrument.

# 9

# Trial By Jury

No freeman shall be taken or imprisoned, or deseized, or outlawed or banished, or anyways destroyed; nor will we pass upon him, or commit him to prison, unless by the legal judgment of his peers, or by the law of the land.

Magna Carta (1215)

William Penn is known to North Americans as the man who founded the state of Pennsylvania. What is generally not known is that as one of two defendants in a trial in England in 1670, he inadvertently contributed to a famous case known as Bushell's case. Bushell's case stands as a landmark in English jurisprudence and established beyond question the independence of the jury.

William Penn was born in 1644, the son of a wealthy British Admiral, Sir William Penn. Sir William had fought in the first Dutch wars of 1652-54 and 1665-67 and also commanded the expedition which captured Jamaica in 1665. In his early teens, William was sent to Chigwell School for a classical education and to his father's annoyance came under Puritan influence. In 1666, his father sent him to Ireland to manage the family estates. There he came under the influence of the Quakers, who were then a despised sect, and he soon became a devoted adherent to their cause and beliefs. He became known as a Quaker preacher and pamphleteer. This devotion, however, soon landed him in jail, and incurred the wrath of his father who threatened to disinherit him. In fact one of his pamphlets caused his arrest and confinement in the Tower of London for eight months without trial. Nevertheless, he became an able and outspoken defender of his new found faith until his death in 1718.

During his life, he published over one hundred publications attacking the doctrines of the established churches and expounding Quaker Puritan morality. That morality was best expressed in his statement that "true Godliness don't turn Men out of the World, but enables them to live better in it, and excites their Endeavours to mend it."

Quakers, like other dissenters, were not popular in England during the reign of the Stuart Kings. To ensure that there was no deviation from the official faith, the authorities were instructed to break up any meeting of Quakers.

On August 14, 1670, the local authorities padlocked the Quaker meeting house in Gracechurch Street in London. Undaunted by their actions, Penn began to preach outside the meeting house. Soon several hundred persons gathered to listen to him. It was not long before Penn and William Mead, another Quaker, were dragged away by the Mayor's men. Ironically neither Penn nor Mead had ever set eyes on each other until they were arrested. They were charged with "unlawfully and tumultously" assembling and addressing the people in Gracechurch Street "whereof a great concourse of people did remain in the street a long time; in contempt of the King and his law; to the great disturbance of his peace; to the great terror of many of his liege people and subjects. . . ."

The trial began before the Recorder (a local barrister appointed to act as judge) and a jury on September 1, 1670 and lasted four days. As was the custom in those days, members of the local government sat with the trial judge. In this case, the Lord Mayor, five aldermen and three sheriffs sat at the judges bench along with the Recorder.

After the charge was read to Penn and Mead, they were asked to plead and each pleaded "not guilty in manner and form." The morning proceeded with the arraignment of the accused and the court was adjourned until the afternoon. That afternoon the trial was again adjourned — this time for two days — while other trials went ahead.

The trial of Penn and Mead started on the morning of September 3, 1670. No sooner had the prisoners entered the dock than an incident happened which set the stage for the many flareups which would occur during the trial. Just before the prisoners had entered court, one of the court officers had removed their hats, probably because Quakers refused to do so. Yet no sooner had they stepped into the prisoner's dock than another court officer ordered them to put their hats back on so that they could remove them in the presence of the judge as a sign of respect. They refused to do so and were subjected to abuse by the Recorder for wearing a hat in the King's Court.

Penn answered him quietly "I know it to be a court and I suppose it is the King's. But I do not think that pulling off our hats shows any respect."

When the Recorder immediately fined them forty marks apiece for contempt, Penn could not restrain himself,

> We came in with our hats off and the Court ordered us to put them on and therefore the Bench ought to be fined rather than Mead and myself.

After a witness testified about the meeting and the people assembled, the Recorder tried to trap William Mead into making an admission and asked if he was there. Mead, however, refused to fall into the trap:

> It is a maxim in your law, nemo tenetur accusare seipsum, which, if it not be true Latin I am sure it is true English, that no man is bound to accuse himself. And why dost thou

offer to ensnare me with such a question? Doth not this show thy malice: is this like unto a judge that ought to be counsel for the prisoner at the bar?

The following exchange then took place between Penn and the Recorder.

PENN: Let me know upon what law you ground my indictment:
RECORDER: Upon the common law.
PENN: Where is the common law?
RECORDER: You must not think that I am able to go back over so many years and over so many adjudged cases which we call common law to satisfy your curiosity.
PENN: The answer, I am sure, is very short of my question; for if it be common law it should not be so hard to produce.

Realizing that the accused were not going to give up their lives without a fight, the judges of the court began to heatedly attack the prisoners. Penn, however, was not intimidated by their authority and fought back:

I design no affront to the court. Only to be heard in my just plea. I must plainly tell you that if you will not let me hear the law which you suggest I have broken, you do at once deny me an acknowledged right, and show to the whole world your resolution to sacrifice the privileges of Englishmen to your sinister and arbitrary designs.

This was too much for the judges whose patience he had finally exhausted. Penn was ordered to be removed from the prisoner's dock and placed in the bail-dock, a cylindrical box in a corner of the courtroom where prisoners were kept until their case was called.

The Lord Mayor now turned his attention to Mead:

You profess yourself a meek man, but deserve to have your tongue cut out for affronting the Court.

The Recorder added a few more threats but Mead was not to be cowed either:

Thou didst promise me I should have fair liberty to be heard. Why may I not have the privilege of an Englishman. I am an Englishman. You should be ashamed of dealing thus with me.

This outburst quickly landed Mead in the bail-dock beside Penn.

The Recorder then summed up to the jury in language that clearly indicated to them that they must convict the two prisoners or suffer the consequences. The jury were then sent out to consider their verdict. But after 1½ hours of deliberating, they could not agree and were brought back into the courtroom. The Recorder, suspecting that one of the jurors, Edward Bushell, was behind the division, threatened to indict him because "you have thrust yourself upon this jury," (meaning that he had deliberately tried to get selected). Bushell replied that he would have willingly got off jury duty but could not.

Under this threat the jury were sent out again to deliberate. After a lengthy deliberation, they returned. This time they gave a verdict finding Penn guilty of only speaking or preaching in Gracechurch Street and declared Mead not guilty. But this was not a legal verdict insofar as Penn was concerned because it did not deal with the charge. Nevertheless, the jury would not budge even though the Recorder refused to accept it. Raging he told them,

> Gentlemen, you shall not be dismissed till we have a verdict that the court will accept; and you shall be locked up, without meat, drink, fire and tobacco. You shall not think thus to abuse the court. We shall have a verdict by the help of God, or you shall starve for it.

However, Penn, who had been allowed to return to court to hear the verdict, insisted that the Court was required to accept the verdict. When the Recorder refused to do so, Penn turned to the jury and appealed to them to hold fast: "You are Englishmen — mind your privilege. Give not away your right." Moved by these words, several members shouted "nor will we ever do it."

To pressure the jury to reach the verdict which they wanted, the Lord Mayor and the Recorder ordered that they be locked up for the night until 7:00 o'clock the next morning without "so much as a chamber pot." The following morning, the jury were returned to the courtroom and directed again to return a verdict of guilty against both prisoners. In order to impress upon the jury their determination to have a verdict of guilty, the Lord Mayor told the foreman of the jury, Edward Bushell, that he would "cut his throat as soon as he could." But, the jury refused to submit to this threat and budge from their verdict of not guilty for Mead and guilty only of "speaking" for Penn.

They were again detained another night without food, water or physical comforts and returned to court the next morning at 7:00. This time they asked that their verdict be returned to them. It was obvious that the jury had changed their verdict. With excitement the clerk of the court asked: "What say you? Is William Penn guilty or not guilty?" This time the verdict was clear: "Not Guilty."

This verdict so enraged the judges that the Recorder immediately fined each member of the jury 40 marks (a substantial sum in those days) and ordered them to be carted off to the infamous Newgate Prison until they paid it. Eight of the jurors relented and decided to pay their fine. But Bushell and three others refused. They wanted to test the legality of their imprisonment. And so, they applied for a writ of *habeas corpus*.

After two months in prison they were released on bail. A year later the Court of Common Pleas rendered a unanimous verdict which said that a jury could not be punished for their verdict. Sir John Vaughan, the Lord

Chief Justice, wrote the judgment. The law was clear he said: "a judge may try to open the eyes of the jurors but not lead them by the nose."

## How Trial By Jury Began

To the ordinary man or woman on the street, trial by jury of someone accused of a crime is considered as the ultimate in fairness and humanity. It envisages a system of justice which tries to ensure that no one accused of a crime will be convicted and punished until a jury of 12 ordinary men and women, randomly selected from the community, has heard and accepted evidence which establishes the guilt of the accused beyond a reasonable doubt. Evidence is expected to be presented fairly and dispassionately by Crown counsel whose only interest is that, as one judge has said, "the right person should be convicted, that the truth should be known and that justice should be done." However, trial by jury as we know it today is really only of recent origin. Trials in the time of William Penn or even a hundred years ago bear very little resemblance to what they are today.

The concept of trial by jury started off differently. It was an invention of the Norman Conquerors, not as a method of trial, but to ensure that persons suspected of crimes were brought to the attention of the authorities. It was also used as a method of obtaining revenue for the Crown. It started in this way.

Members of a community were originally summoned before a King's officer, the Coroner (or Crowner) to provide all sorts of information about the community. That information was given under oath, a requirement that only the King could enforce. Those summoned were not initially used as a jury to settle disputes. Disputes were usually settled on the battlefield or by the ordeal, a system in which the accused appealed to the supernatural to deliver him from death or burning and thus prove his innocence.

By the end of the 12th century, this group of citizens or jurors, summoned to provide information about their community, now began to be used to report any of their neighbours whom they suspected of committing crimes. When Pope Innocent III prohibited trial by ordeal at the Fourth Lateran Council in 1215, English courts were forced to devise a new method of trying offenders. They naturally turned to the jury which had accused the prisoner. The prisoner was asked if he was willing to be tried by his neighbours and "to put himself upon his country." Because conviction meant death by hanging or burning and the loss to his heirs by forfeiture of his lands and chattels, many refused to answer. If an accused refused, he was usually kept in prison until he agreed. To speed up the process, a system was later devised known as "peine forte et dure" whereby heavy weights were placed on the prisoner's chest until he agreed to plead or expired.

Complaints, however, began to arise from prisoners that they were being tried by the same jury that was accusing them. By the beginning of the 14th century, the practice arose of adding fresh jurors. Eventually in 1352, during the reign of Edward III, a statute was passed allowing the prisoner to challenge any juror who had been a member of the original indicting body.

When a juror is selected today, it is expected that he knows nothing about the case against the accused. Indeed, an accused is entitled to an impartial jury and has the right to challenge any juror who is not. That is not the way it was for a number of centuries after the system of trial by jury was introduced.

In the small parochial English communities of the Middle Ages, everyone knew everything about his neighbour. The jurors were expected to know all about the prisoner and often acted only on local gossip. The Crown could call witnesses to substantiate the allegations in the indictment if it wanted but it was not necessary to do so. The jury were entitled to return a verdict of guilty simply on their own knowledge of the charges against the accused.

On the other hand, the accused was not entitled to call any evidence in his defence nor was he entitled to testify himself. An interesting example of this was the case of Sir Nicholas Throckmorton in 1554. Throckmorton, who was charged with publishing articles of a seditious nature, asked the Court if John Fitzwilliams should be called "to depose in this matter what he can." When John Fitzwilliams drew to the bar and presented himself to give his evidence on behalf of Throckmorton in open court, the following exchange took place.

> ATTORNEY: (For the Crown) I pray you, my lords, suffer him not to be sworn, neither to speak; we have nothing to do with him.
> THROCKMORTON: Why should he not be suffered to tell the truth: And why be ye not so well contented to hear truth from me as untruth against me?
> MASTER OF THE ROLLS (The judge): Who called you hither, Fitzwilliams, or commanded you to speak: You are a very busy officer?
> THROCKMORTON: I called him, and do humbly desire that he may speak and be heard as well as Vaughan, or else I am not indifferently used; especially seeing Master Attorney doth so press this matter against me.
> PRIVY COUNCILLOR (one of the judges): Go your ways, Fitzwilliams, the court hath nothing to do with you. Peradventure you would not be so ready in a good cause.

John Fitzwilliams was not allowed to give evidence on behalf of the defence.

Not only was the prisoner not allowed to call evidence for the defence, he was not entitled to have a lawyer to represent him in court. This was particularly unfair because he often had to face several lawyers presenting the case for the Crown.

At the same time, the prisoner was required to answer the allegations contained in the indictment which was often a lengthy and complex document. To make matters worse, the indictment was drafted in Latin at a time when most people could hardly read or write the English language. Confined to prison until his trial, a person accused of a crime was afforded little opportunity to present a proper defence to the charges against him.

This situation continued until the end of the 17th century when persons charged with serious crimes were finally allowed to call witnesses in their defence, although the witnesses were not usually allowed to give such evidence under oath. This reduced the value of the testimony when weighed against the sworn evidence of the Crown witnesses.

It was not until the next century that a prisoner was entitled to have a lawyer to represent him. Initially his counsel could only argue points of law. However, by 1760, the courts began to allow defence counsel to cross-examine witnesses but they were not allowed to address the jury. It was not until 1836, exactly 150 years ago, that an accused was eventually given the full right to counsel. But the most curious rule of all was the rule that a prisoner was not entitled to give sworn evidence himself from the witness box, although he was entitled to give an unsworn statement from the prisoner's dock. Even when the Criminal Evidence Act of 1898 finally gave prisoners that right, there were many against it. Mr. Justice Avory, known as one of the greatest experts in the criminal law, was against it. He pointed out:

> Before the Act no one ever lost sight of that grand principle of our criminal law that no man is liable to be convicted unless the prosecution has satisfied the jury beyond reasonable doubt of his guilt. . . . The moment the law was altered there was the danger that if a man went into the witness-box the jury might think it was for him to establish his innocence.

Over two centuries ago the great English jurist, Sir William Blackstone, in his Commentaries on the Laws of England, described the fundamental importance of trial by jury in these now classic words:

> [S]ince, in times of difficulty and danger, more is to be apprehended from the violence and partiality of judges appointed by the crown, in suits between the King and the subject, than in disputes between one individual and another, to settle the metes and boundaries of private property. Our law has therefore wisely placed this strong and twofold barrier of a presentment and a trial by jury, between the liberties of the people, and the prerogative of the crown. It was necessary for preserving the admirable balance of our constitution, to vest the executive power of the laws in the prince: and yet this power might be dangerous and destructive to the very constitution, if exerted without check or control by justices oyer and terminer occasionally named by the crown; who might then, as in France or Turkey imprison, despatch or exile any man that was obnoxious to the government, by an instant declaration, that such is their will and pleasure. But the founders of the English law have with excellent forcast contrived, that no man should be called to answer to the King for any capital crime, unless upon the preparatory accusation of twelve or more of his fellow subjects, the grand jury: and that

the truth of every accusation, whether preferred in the shape of an indictment, information or appeal, should afterwards be confirmed by the unanimous suffrage of twelve of his equals and neighbours, indifferently chosen, and superior to all suspicion. So that the liberties of England cannot but subsist so long as this palladium remains sacred and inviolate; not only from all open attacks, (which none will be so hardy as to make) but also from all secret machinations which may sap and undermine it; by introducing new and arbitrary methods of trial, by justices of the peace, commissioners of the revenue, and courts of conscience. And however convenient these may appear at first, (as doubtless all arbitrary powers, well executed, are the most convenient) yet let it be remembered, that delays, and little inconveniences in the forms of justice, are the price that all free nations must pay for their liberty in more substantial matters; that these inroads upon this sacred bulwark of the nation are fundamentally opposite to the spirit of our constitution; and that, though begun at trifles, the precedent may gradually increase and spread, to the utter disuse of juries in questions of the most momentous concern.

The concern expressed by Blackstone about the partiality of judges in favour of the Crown was not without foundation. Until the Act of Settlement in 1701, judges were appointed and removed by the King willy nilly unless they did his bidding. Even the great chief justice, Sir Edward Coke, who fought so valiantly for the independence of the judiciary, was eventually brought to his knees and dismissed from his office by King James I.

Judges were generally able to persuade the jury to reach a desired verdict by threats and bullying tactics. To ensure that the verdict was rendered quickly and with little time for reflection, it was the practice of the judge to order the sheriff to lock up the jury without food, water, heat or chamberpot until they reached their decision. As an added measure to ensure that juries did their bidding and convicted the prisoner, particularly where the crime alleged involved an attack on the Crown, judges developed two methods to control a jury's verdict: the attaint and the fine.

The writ of attaint was usually used to deal with a civil jury that had rendered a verdict that was not favourable to the judge. What the trial judge did was to empanel a larger jury made up of 24 men of higher standing than the first to try the case again. If the second jury rendered a verdict that was contrary to the first, then the first jury was found guilty of perjury and punished by fine or imprisonment; the first judgment was also reversed.

However, as jurors began to hear evidence from witnesses rather than to rely on their own knowledge or suspicion, it was recognized that an attaint jury could not reverse an earlier verdict unless it was based on exactly the same evidence. Furthermore, attaint juries became more reluctant to render a different verdict when they knew that it would cause the first jury to be severely punished. Although attaint juries became obsolete by the end of the 15th century, they were not formally abolished until 1825.

In the 15th century, judges tried to introduce a more effective way of coercing the jury to reach a certain verdict. Since judges had developed the right to control and punish persons who brought the administration of justice into disrepute by the power of contempt, the threat of contempt was now used upon jurors who rendered an unpopular verdict. The power was reinforced by a statute enacted in 1534, during the reign of Henry VIII, which authorized the judge to punish a jury which gave "an untrue verdict against the king, contrary to good and pregnant evidence ministered to them."

And so it was that juries who rendered an unpopular verdict were punished and imprisoned. In the case of Sir Nicholas Throckmorton referred to earlier, the jury acquitted him, notwithstanding that they were not allowed to hear from Fitzwilliams or any other witness favourable to the defence. For their troubles the jury were fined and imprisoned, the foreman himself being fined the enormous sum of £2,000. This practice continued until the famous opinion of Chief Justice Vaughan in 1670 in Bushell's case.

The judges soon turned to another method of controlling juries. Wealthy land-owners were placed on a special panel of jurors for the trial of charges of sedition and unlawful assembly. Through the use of these panels, special juries could be selected who would be expected to find against any subversive movements.

The Revolution of 1688 ended this practice. In the following year, the Bill of Rights abolished the practice of selecting as jurors "partial, corrupt and unqualified persons."

## Trial By Jury In America

Trial by jury was introduced to North America by the English colonists. The famous Declaration of the Thirteen United States of America in Congress on July 4, 1776 listed a number of grievances against the arbitrary rule of King George II. Among those grievances were,

He has obstructed the Administration of Justice, by refusing his Assent to Laws for establishing Judiciary powers.

He has made Judges dependent on his Will alone, for the tenure of their offices, and the amount and payment of their salaries.

He has combined with others to subject us to a jurisdiction foreign to our constitution and unacknowledged by our laws, giving his Assent to their Acts of Pretended Legislation:—. . .

For depriving us in many cases of the benefits of Trial by Jury. . . .

Article III of the Constitution of the United States which became effective March 4, 1789 now ensured that,

The Trial of all Crimes, except in Cases of Impeachment, shall be by Jury. . . .

The Sixth Amendment of the Constitution passed by Congress on September 25, 1789 went on to confirm that,

In all criminal prosecutions, the accused shall enjoy the right to a speedy and public trial, by an impartial jury of the State and district wherein the crime shall have been committed, which districts shall have been previously ascertained by law, and to be informed of the nature and cause of the accusation; to be confronted with the witnesses against him; to have compulsory process for obtaining witnesses in his favour, and to have the assistance of counsel for his defence.

## Trial By Jury In Canada

Trial by jury was introduced as part of the common law of England to the colonies of Prince Edward Island, Nova Scotia and New Brunswick. Although Quebec fell to the British conquest in 1760, it was not until the Royal Proclamation of 1763, introducing the common law of England as the law of Quebec, that trial by jury was given to the new colony for both criminal and civil trials. However, in 1774, the British Parliament restored French law in civil matters by the Quebec Act; thus trial by jury in civil matters was abolished in that province. Following the American Revolution, the United Empire Loyalists returning to Canada objected to the denial of trial by jury in civil cases. The result was the Constitutional Act of 1791 which separated Quebec into the provinces of Upper and Lower Canada. One of the first Acts passed by the new legislature for Upper Canada was the introduction of the common law of England and the right of trial by jury in criminal and civil cases.

The British North America Act, 1867 entrusted jurisdiction over "The Criminal Law, except the Constitution of Courts of Criminal Jurisdiction but including the Procedure in Criminal matters . . ." to the Parliament of Canada. In 1893, Parliament introduced the Criminal Code which preserved the right of trial by judge and jury with respect to all offences of a serious nature.

Under the common law of England, all crimes fell into two categories. The first was indictable offences; they included treasons, felonies and misdemeanours. The second category involved petty offences; they were tried summarily by justices of the peace sitting without a jury.

The Criminal Code of 1893 abolished the various classifications of crimes. All crimes now fell into two categories; indictable offences and summary conviction offences. That distinction was carried over into the revised Criminal Code of 1955. There was added, however, a third classification which has been called hybrid or dual offences. Such offences depend upon how the Crown Attorney elects to proceed at trial.

All summary conviction offences must be tried by a summary conviction court which usually consists of a provincial court judge or justice of the peace presiding without a jury. However, not all indictable offences may be tried by a jury. A provincial court judge has the absolute jurisdiction to hear certain offences such as theft, fraud or possession of stolen goods valued at $1000 or less or offences involving gaming or bawdy houses where the maximum penalty which he may impose is not more than two years' imprisonment. In all other instances, with the exception of murder, treason and other offences against the security of the state and piracy, an accused has the right to be tried by a judge and jury or by a judge or provincial court judge sitting alone without a jury. Where the crime is murder, treason or piracy, the accused must be tried by a jury, unless the Crown consents to trial by a superior court judge sitting alone.

There are some people who believe that the right to be tried by a jury of one's peers is too wide in Canada and should be limited to only serious offences such as murder, treason, piracy, armed robbery, rape etc. Others believe that where the crimes alleged are assaults upon the police, the right to trial by jury should be removed. Fortunately, this assault on the jury system has been resisted by everyone who believes in liberty. In 1956, Lord Devlin, delivering the annual Hamlyn Lectures, described the importance of trial by jury in these terms:

> Each jury is a little parliament. The jury sense is the parliamentary sense. I cannot see the one dying and the other surviving. The first object of any tyrant in Whitehall would be to make Parliament utterly subservient to his will; and the next to overthrow or diminish trial by jury, for no tyrant could afford to leave a subject's freedom in the hands of twelve of his countrymen. So that trial by jury is more than an instrument of justice and more than one wheel of the constitution: it is the lamp that shows that freedom lives.

To Lord Devlin, the jury served two very essential purposes. The first was as a safeguard of the independence and quality of judges.

> Judges are appointed by the executive and I do not know of any better way of appointing them. Our history has shown that the executive has found it much easier to find judges who will do what it wants than it has to find amenable juries. Blackstone, whose time was not so far removed from that of the Stuarts thought of the jury as a safeguard against "the violence and partiality of judges appointed by the Crown."
> Commenting on that in 1784, Mr. Justice Willes said: "I am sure no danger of this sort is to be apprehended from the judges of the present age: but in our determinations it will be prudent to look forward into futurity." Although in 1956 we may claim that "futurity" has not yet arrived, it still remains prudent to look forward into it.

The second purpose was that,

> It gives protection against laws which the ordinary man may regard as harsh and oppressive. I do not mean by that no more than that it is a protection against tyranny. It

is that: but it is also an insurance that the criminal law will conform to the ordinary man's idea of what is fair and just. If it does not, the jury will not be a party to its enforcement. They have in the past used their power of acquittal to defeat the full operation of laws which they thought to be too hard. I dare say that the cases in which a jury defies the law are very rare. Juries do not deliberately marshal legal considerations on one side and broader considerations of justice and mercy on the other and bring them into conflict on the field of conscience. Their minds are not trained to the making of an orderly separation and opposition; they are more likely to allow one set of considerations to act upon the other in such a way as to confuse the issues. One way or the other they are prone to give effect to their repugnance to a law by refusing to convict under it, and no one can say them nay. The small body of men, who under modern conditions constitute the effective body of legislators, have to bear this in mind. It affects the character of the laws they make, for it is no use making laws which will not be enforced. They may put it down to the perversity of juries, though for my part I think that if there is a law which the jury-man constantly shows by his verdicts that he dislikes, it is worth examining the law to see if there is something wrong with it rather than with the juryman. . . . The ordinary member of Parliament participates in law-making by helping with the details, but in all matters of principle he is obedient — subject to his conscience — to the party whip, which is the executive. The executive knows that in dealing with the liberty of the subject it must not do anything which would seriously disturb the conscience of the average member of Parliament or of the average juryman. I know of no other real checks that exist today upon the power of the executive. (pp. 160-62)

# The Charter Enshrines Trial By Jury

Parliament undoubtedly recognized the importance of trial by jury when it decided to enshrine that right in the Charter of Rights and Freedoms. Section 11(*f*) provides:

11. Any person charged with an offence has the right

(*f*) except in the case of an offence under military law tried before a military tribunal, to the benefit of trial by jury where the maximum punishment for the offence is imprisonment for five years or a more severe punishment.

Section 11(*f*) denies a soldier the right to trial by jury where he has committed an offence under military law. This exclusion is easily understandable. The ordinary member of the public does not appreciate the importance of discipline which is so essential to an effective army. The section, however, does not include young offenders who may be confined for periods in excess of five years, or persons charged with contempt of court. Although there have been applications to the court seeking jury trials for young offenders, there has been no definitive answer to date on this issue.

In 1972 the Bail Reform Act was passed by the Parliament of Canada. Its objective was to reduce pre-trial detention. It imposes on a peace officer who arrests an accused or the officer in charge of the lock-up, the duty of releasing the accused unless there are reasonable and probable grounds to believe it is necessary in the public interest to detain him in custody or that if released, he will fail to appear in court. The result is that many persons who would have, prior to the legislation, been kept in custody until trial are now given their freedom pending their trial.

However, it was discovered after four years that many people who had been released were not showing up for their trial. The result was that occasionally a panel of jurors who had been summoned to try the accused had to be sent home until the accused could be found. In other instances, the accused appeared for his trial and a jury was selected. Then, as the trial progressed, the accused may have decided not to appear which meant that the jury selected had to be sent home until the accused showed up or was arrested.

In 1976, Parliament decided that it could best prevent this abuse of the Bail Reform Act and save the expense and inconvenience of abortive jury trials by passing legislation which would deny an absconding accused the right to trial by jury. Section 526.1 of the Code was introduced. It imposed upon an accused, who failed to appear or to remain in attendance for his trial, the obligation of satisfying a judge that there was a legitimate excuse for his failure to appear or remain in attendance, otherwise he automatically lost his right to trial by jury.

Shortly after the enactment of the Charter of Rights and Freedoms, section 526.1 came under attack as a denial of the right to trial by jury. In the province of Alberta, it was decided in *Regina v. Crate* that section 526.1 did not infringe section 11(*f*) of the Charter. Mr. Justice Lieberman who delivered the judgment of the court ruled that section 526.1 was a reasonable limitation and demonstrably justified in a free and democratic society. As far as he was concerned,

> It is eminently reasonable and completely justifiable to say to an accused who has called upon the State to empanel a jury and, more importantly, called upon his fellow citizens to answer their duty to appear in order to serve as jurors, that he cannot impose that obligation a second time unless he meets the requirements set out in section 526.1.

In Ontario, the Court of Appeal has not agreed with that view. In *Regina v. Bryant*, the Court felt that section 526.1 cannot be justified as a reasonable limit on the right to trial by jury. Parliament has no right to deny Charter rights to those who abuse the judicial process. If that were so then a Charter right would be a mere privilege which "a government can take away for improper conduct rather than as entrenched rights beyond the reach of government."

Mr. Justice Blair who delivered the main judgment of the Court noted that there are other provisions of the Code which can impose penalties on those who fail to show up for trial. Once re-arrested, an accused can be kept in custody subject to being released only by the judge who presides over his trial. In addition, he can be charged with the offence of failing to appear and is subject to a penalty of up to two years' imprisonment.

As noted earlier, Sir William Blackstone cautioned us to be vigilant against "these inroads upon this sacred bulwark of the nation." In words appropriate to repeat,

> delays and little inconveniences in the forms of justice are the price that all free nations must pay for their liberty in more substantial matters. . . .

# 10

# Right To Counsel

The most innocent man, pressed by the awful solemnities of public accusation and trial, may be incapable of supporting his own cause. He may be utterly unfit to cross-examine the witnesses against him, to point out the contradictions or defects of their testimony, and to counteract it by properly introducing it and applying his own.

William Rawle, Philadelphia (1825)

The test of the moral quality of a civilization is its treatment of the weak and powerless.

Judge Jerome Frank, *United States v. Murphy* (1955)

On August 4, 1961, Clarence Earl Gideon stood before Judge McCrary, Jr. of the Fourteen Judicial Circuit of Florida to begin his trial on a charge of breaking and entering with intent to commit a misdemeanour, to wit, petty larceny. It was alleged that he had broken into the Bay Harbour Pool Room in Panama City, Florida, and had taken a bottle of wine which was 4/5ths full, 12 bottles of coca cola, 12 cans of beer, about $5.00 from the cigarette machine and $60.00 from the juke box.

Gideon was not a new-comer to the judicial system. He had been convicted of four previous felonies and had spent much of his life in and out of prisons. That may have been why he looked much older than his 51 years. But he had never been a really professional criminal or a man of violence. He seemed unable to keep a steady job; and so, to support himself over the years, he lived by his wits through gambling and petty thievery. At the time of his arraignment, he was married for a second time. He and his wife had six children, three of which were his.

When Gideon appeared before Judge McCrary, he was not represented by counsel. It was probably because of his numerous brushes with the law that he recognized his need for one to represent him at his trial. The proceedings that followed went like this:

THE COURT: The next case on the docket is the case of the State of Florida, Plaintiff, versus Clarence Earl Gideon, Defendant. What says the State, are you ready to go to trial in this case?

MR. HARRIS: (William E. Harris, Assistant State Attorney). The State is ready, Your Honour.

THE COURT: What says the Defendant? Are you ready to go to trial?

THE DEFENDANT: I am not ready, Your Honour.

THE COURT: Did you plead not guilty to this charge by reason of insanity?

THE DEFENDANT: No sir.

THE COURT: Why aren't you ready?

THE DEFENDANT: I have no counsel.

THE COURT: Why do you not have counsel: Did you not know that your case was set for trial today?

THE DEFENDANT: Yes, sir, I knew that it was set for today.

THE COURT: Why, then, did you not secure counsel and be prepared to go to trial?

The defendant answered the Court's question, but spoke in such low tones that it was not audible.

THE COURT: Come closer up, Mr. Gideon, I can't understand you, I don't know what you said and the Reporter didn't understand you either.

At this point the Defendant arose from his chair where he was seated at the counsel table and walked up and stood directly in front of the bench facing His Honour Judge McCrary

THE COURT: Now tell us what you said again, so we can understand you, please.

THE DEFENDANT: Your Honour, I said: I request this Court to appoint counsel to represent me in this trial.

THE COURT: Mr. Gideon, I am sorry, but I cannot appoint counsel to represent you in this case. Under the laws of the State of Florida, the only time the court can appoint counsel to represent a Defendant is when that person is charged with a capital offense. I am sorry, but I will have to deny your request to appoint counsel to defend you in this case.

THE DEFENDANT: The United States Supreme Court says I am entitled to be represented by counsel.

THE COURT: Let the record show that the Defendant has asked the court to appoint counsel to represent him in this trial and the court denied the request and informed the Defendant that the only time the Court could appoint counsel to represent a defendant was in cases where the defendant was charged with a capital offense. The Defendant stated to the court that the United States Supreme Court said he was entitled to it.

Judge McCrary ordered the trial to proceed and advised Mr. Gideon that he had a right to challenge the jurors. He replied, "they suit me alright, Your Honour" and the jury was soon selected. Only two witnesses were called for the prosecution. The chief witness, Henry Cook, testified that he was outside the Bay Harbour Pool Room at 5:30 in the morning on June 3, 1961, and saw Gideon inside. After watching him through the window for a few minutes Cook said, that he saw Gideon come out with a pint of wine in his hand, make a telephone call at the street corner and then in due course get into a taxi. He then went to the pool room and saw that it had been broken into. The front was off the cigarette machine and a money box was lying on a pool table.

Gideon called eight witnesses on his behalf, none of whom could offer any real assistance. He did not testify himself but spoke to the jury at the end of the case for approximately 11 minutes, emphasizing his innocence. The jury eventually returned with a verdict of guilty. Judge McCrary adjourned the case for three weeks to get a report on Gideon's past history. On August 25, without asking Gideon whether he had anything to say, the judge sentenced him to five years' imprisonment, the maximum penalty for the offence.

While Gideon was in prison, he wrote to the Supreme Court of the United States and asked to be allowed to petition the Court to grant him a new trial because he had been denied the right to counsel. He relied upon the Fourteenth Amendment to the Constitution which provides that, "no State shall . . . deprive any person of life, liberty, or property, without due process of law." He felt that he had been denied "due process" because he had been denied counsel. Six months after receiving his application, the Court agreed to hear his appeal.

Had Gideon been denied the right to counsel? Did the Constitution of the United States guarantee him the right to have counsel represent him at his trial? Gideon obviously believed that it did. However, 20 years earlier the Supreme Court of the United States had decided in a controversial decision — *Betts v. Brady* — that the Constitution of the United States did not guarantee everyone the right to counsel in every case. But before looking at that decision, we should take ourselves back a few hundred years and see how the right to counsel developed under the English common law.

## Right To Counsel At Common Law

As was pointed out in the last chapter, the ordinary member of the public's conception of a modern criminal trial with on one side, a strong but fairminded prosecutor presenting the evidence of the Crown or State, and on the other, a fearless and passionate defence counsel attacking the evidence, and in the middle an impartial judge, is just a little over a century and a half old. If we were fortunate enough to be transported back in time two or three hundred years, we would observe a system of trial that would shock even the most arch-conservative.

An accused charged with a crime was generally kept in custody, secluded from family and friends until the day of his trial. He would often hear the accusations against him for the first time when the indictment was read in court. Even when the indictment was finally read to him, he could not usually understand it since it was usually drafted in Latin. If he was charged with a misdemeanour (that is, a minor crime), he was allowed representation by counsel. But if the charge was treason or a felony (that is, a capital offence, and most offences such as theft and burglary were felonies), he was not allowed to have counsel to cross-examine witnesses, although some judges did allow counsel to argue points of law for the accused. This curious distinction was probably based on the theory that the more serious the crime, the less chance there should be of an acquittal.

Until 1640, an accused was not even allowed to call witnesses on his behalf if he was charged with a felony; and, when this was eventually permitted, those witnesses were not even allowed to give their evidence under oath. He himself could not give evidence in his own defence, a practice which was not changed until 1898, less than one hundred years ago.

Why was there such a reluctance to give an accused the advantage of properly defending himself? The answer is probably best summed up in these lines:

> For lest the sturdy criminal false witnesses should bring
> His witnesses were not allowed to swear to anything,
> And lest the wily advocate of the Court should overreach
> His advocate was not allowed the privilege of speech.
> Yet, such was the humanity and wisdom of the law
> That if in the indictment there appeared to be a flaw,
> The Court assigned him Counsellors to argue on the doubt,
> Provided he himself had first contrived to point it out
> Yet lest their mildness should by some be craftily abused,
> To show him the indictment they most steadily refused,
> But still that he might understand the nature of the charge,
> The same was, in the latin tongue, read out to him at large!

An accused might be expected to face no fewer than four or five eminent counsel for the Crown — a situation quite dangerous when one considers that he did not even know the case against him until the witnesses were called. Often the judge would harangue him to confess his guilt after a witness for the Crown had testified and this might be accompanied by the verbal attacks of Crown counsel.

It was not until just over 200 years ago in 1760 that the courts finally began to allow an accused counsel to cross-examine witnesses in capital cases but counsel was not entitled to address the jury. In fact, it was just 150 years ago, in 1836, that full right to counsel was eventually given to an accused by statute.

## Right To Counsel In America

Those who had left England to settle in the New World and to form the First Union of Thirteen Colonies of the United States were quick to reject the harsh system of justice under which they had laboured, particularly those who had been prosecuted for expressing their religious beliefs. When the First Congress of the United States passed the first ten amendments to the Constitution (often referred to as the Bill of Rights), the Sixth provided that,

> In all criminal prosecutions, the accused shall . . . have the assistance of counsel for his defence.

This was a clear rejection of the old common law rule preventing defence counsel in felony and treason trials. In time, it also came to mean that the court was required to provide counsel to an accused who was unable to pay for one himself. But the Sixth Amendment only applied to prosecutions conducted by the federal government; and, under the American Constitution, it was the states and not the federal government who had jurisdiction over crimes committed within the state. Although most states had rejected the common law rule and permitted an accused the right to retain counsel, there was no obligation to provide one where an accused was indigent. This effectively meant that only those who could afford to hire a lawyer were entitled "to have the assistance of counsel for his defense."

Indigent persons now turned to the Fourteenth Amendment for assistance. That amendment provides ". . . nor shall any State deprive any person of life, liberty or property, without due process of law. . . ." Could a person who was prosecuted by the state for a criminal offence demand the right to be represented by a lawyer and require the state to provide him one where he had no funds because the failure to do so deprived him of the right to "due process"? The first important decision on this question was the Scottsboro case, *Powell v. Alabama* in 1931. There seven Negro youths were convicted of raping two white girls. The trial had been conducted in three separate proceedings. Each proceeding took a single day. Under Alabama law, the juries voted for the death penalty and each accused had been sentenced to death.

The issue before the Supreme Court of the United States was whether or not they had had effective assistance of counsel. Local members of the bar had been appointed to defend the accused who were tried six days after their indictment. When one remembers that this was 1932 and that two white girls had been allegedly raped by seven Negro boys it is understandable why the atmosphere was very tense and hostile. In fact the militia had been called in to assist the sheriff, who was fearful of a lynching. In the words of Justice Sutherland of the Supreme Court of the United States, the "defendants, young, ignorant, illiterate, surrounded by hostile sentiment, haled back and forth under guards of soldiers, charged with an atrocious crime regarded with especial horror in the community where they were tried, were thus put to peril. . . ."

Justice Sutherland conceded that the Sixth Amendment did not afford the accused the protection they needed. However, he was of the view that the due process clause of the Fourteenth Amendment meant that an accused person was entitled to a "hearing"; and it was fundamental to a meaningful hearing that there be counsel.

Justice Sutherland summed up the dilemma of the unrepresented defendants in these words,

> The right to be heard would be, in many cases, of little avail if it did not comprehend the right to be heard by counsel. Even the intelligent and educated layman has small and

some times no skill in the science of law. If charged with a crime, he is incapable, generally, of determining for himself whether the indictment is good or bad. He is unfamiliar with the rules of evidence. Left without the aid of counsel he may be put on trial without a proper charge, and convicted upon incompetent evidence, or evidence irrelevant to the issue or otherwise inadmissible. He lacks both the skill and knowledge adequately to prepare his defense, even though he have a perfect one. He requires the guiding hand of counsel at every step of the proceedings against him. Without it, though he be not guilty, he faces the danger of conviction because he does not know how to establish his innocence. If that be true of men of intelligence, how much more true is it of the ignorant and illiterate, or those of feeble intellect.

In his view, the necessity of counsel was so vital and imperative that the failure of the trial court to make an effective appointment of counsel was a denial of due process with the meaning of the Fourteenth Amendment.

But Justice Sutherland added a caveat to his judgment, which told future courts to move slowly and cautiously. This decision was limited to the particular facts of that case. It was not intended to direct lower courts to provide indigent persons with counsel in all cases. Nevertheless there were attempts over the next three decades to persuade the Supreme Court to do just that. All attempts were unsuccessful. For example, in 1942, the case of *Betts v. Brady* came before the Supreme Court. Betts had been charged with robbery and had raised the defence of alibi. Like Gideon, he had sought and been denied counsel and then had conducted his own trial.

A petition for *habeas corpus* was denied by the Maryland Court of Appeal. Chief Judge Bond had concluded that the trial was routine, a simple affair, so that "in this case it must be said that there was little for counsel to do on either side." It was argued before the Supreme Court of the United States that the lack of counsel denied the accused his right to due process. But again the Court, in a six-to-three majority decision, agreed with Chief Judge Bond. It reaffirmed the rule that whether counsel should be appointed depended upon the facts of each and every case.

Although only 30 years had passed from the time that *Powell v. Alabama* was heard by the Supreme Court of the United States in 1931 and *Gideon v. Wainwright* appeared on the docket in 1961, many things had occurred which would change the American judicial system. One of the most important of all was the appointment of Earl Warren as Chief Justice of the United States in 1952. Within a few years, the Court, under his influence, reshaped the criminal justice system in the United States. Known as the Warren Court, the Supreme Court began to look more to the needs of those who found themselves before the courts rather than to the precedents of the past. How could anyone accused of a crime exercise those rights guaranteed to him by the Constitution if he could not afford to hire a lawyer to tell him what his rights were?

Abe Fortas, a prominent Washington lawyer, was appointed by the Supreme Court to argue the appeal for Gideon. Fortas, who was destined to be appointed to that court four years later, argued passionately that Gideon should have been assigned a lawyer to defend him:

> Under our adversary system of justice, how can our civilized nation pretend that there is a fair trial without the counsel for the prosecution doing all he can within the limits of decency, and counsel for the defence doing his best within the same limits, and from that clash will emerge the truth? ... I think there is a tendency to forget what happens to these poor, miserable, indigent people — in these strange and awesome circumstances. Sometimes in this Court there is a tendency to forget what happens downstairs. ... I was reminded the other night, as I was pondering this case, of Clarence Darrow when he was prosecuted for trying to fix a jury. The first thing he realized was that he needed a lawyer — he, one of the country's greatest criminal lawyers. ...

His plea did not go unheeded. All nine judges of the Court agreed with him. Mr. Justice Black who delivered the main judgment said:

> [R]eason and reflection require us to recognize that in our adversary system of criminal justice, any person haled into court, who is too poor to hire a lawyer, cannot be assured a fair trial unless counsel is provided for him. This seems to us to be an obvious truth. Governments, both state and federal, quite properly spend vast sums of money to establish machinery to try defendants accused of crime. Lawyers to prosecute are everywhere deemed essential to protect the public's interest in an orderly society. Similarly, there are few defendants charged with crime, few indeed, who fail to hire the best lawyers they can get to prepare and present their defenses. That government hires lawyers to prosecute and defendants who have the money hire lawyers to defend are the strongest indication of the widespread belief that lawyers in criminal courts are necessities, not luxuries. The right of one charged with crime to counsel may not be deemed fundamental and essential to fair trials in some countries, but it is in ours.

## Gideon's Re-Trial

Was legal counsel able to assist Clarence Earl Gideon when he appeared for his new trial before Judge McCrary? The publicity surrounding the now famous case had brought Gideon the offer of two experienced criminal lawyers from the Florida Civil Liberties Union. Gideon, however, told Judge McCrary that he did not want either of them. In fact, he didn't want another lawyer at all. He wanted to defend himself.

But Judge McCrary was not about to give Gideon the chance to complain again that he had been denied counsel. This time he told him that he was going to have a lawyer represent him whether he wanted one or not. Gideon indicated that he had confidence in a local lawyer, Fred Turner. And so Judge McCrary appointed Turner to represent Gideon at his new trial.

The second trial began at 9.00 a.m. on August 5, 1963. This time the state was represented by three lawyers — the original prosecutor, Assistant State Attorney William E. Harris, his boss J. Frank Adams, the State Attorney for the circuit, and J. Paul Griffith, an assistant. Gideon was represented by only one counsel, Fred Turner.

Henry Cook again testified as he had in the first trial — he had observed Gideon inside the poolroom and then watched him leave to make a telephone call at a telephone booth. This time, however, Turner wanted to know what Cook was doing outside the poolroom at 5.30 in the morning. Cook replied that he had been at a dance 60 miles away and he had asked his friends to drop him off there because "I was going to hang around there till the poolroom opened up — seven o'clock."

Turner saw his opportunity to move in: — How could he see into the poolroom past the advertising boards on the windows? — Why did he not call the police then or even later? — Had he ever been convicted of a felony? (Cook had denied it at the first trial — now he admitted he had pleaded guilty to car theft).

Then came the suggestion — ". . . did you go into the Bay Harbor Poolroom? Did you all get a six-pack of beer out of there?" Cook answered no to both questions.

This time the defence called only two witnesses. One was Gideon. He denied knowing anything about the break-in. At 4.20 p.m. the jury was sent out to deliberate. One hour and five minutes later, they were back with a verdict of "Not Guilty." When Judge McCrary inquired — "So say you all?" they all nodded agreement.

## When Does Right To Counsel Begin

Over the last quarter century, an equally important question has perplexed the courts. Is an accused entitled to be represented by a lawyer at an earlier stage than the trial? If he is, at what stage? At the time there is a formal written accusation made against him; or earlier such as, at the stage of the police interrogation?

Unfortunately, we sometimes forget that police officers are not a foreign army controlled by a foreign state. They are our representatives, hired and paid by the people we elect to represent us. They are there to protect us. They are also there to solve crimes and to prosecute the person believed to have committed that crime.

The ordinary citizen has two rights. One is the right to be protected by the police from the aggression of others. He is also entitled, if suspected of having committed an act of aggression against someone else, of having his constitutional rights respected.

One of the most important investigative tools that a police officer has is the interrogation process. Through interrogation of a suspected offender, the police officer may obtain a confession of guilt or other evidence to strengthen his case against the suspect. He may also obtain information which will point guilt to someone else. The officer, however, knows that the presence of defence counsel during interrogation will obstruct his efforts. The first thing counsel will do is tell his client to say nothing until he has had the opportunity to find out what is the evidence against him. When defence counsel does so, he is not obstructing the administration of justice. He is only carrying out his professional duty to his client. It was these two competing interests — the right of society to investigate crime versus the right of every citizen to have his constitutional right to counsel respected — that faced the Supreme Court of the United States in *Miranda v. Arizona* in 1966.

Ernesto Miranda had been convicted of kidnapping and rape in Arizona. He had been arrested and taken to an interrogation room by the police where he was questioned without being advised of the right to have a lawyer present during the interrogation. Two hours later, the police had a confession from him and that confession was admitted into evidence over Miranda's objection.

Before the Supreme Court of the United States, Miranda's lawyer argued that by failing to advise him of his right to have counsel present during his interrogation, he had been denied the right "to have the assistance of counsel for his defence" guaranteed by the Sixth Amendment. It was also argued that to interrogate a man without the presence of his lawyer breached his right not to "be compelled in any criminal case to be a witness against himself" a right guaranteed by the Fifth Amendment.

During the course of argument, Duane R. Nedrud, who presented a brief as *amicus curiae* on behalf of the National District Attorney's Association, made this submission:

> If we are talking about equality between the rich and the poor, we are striving for a worthy object. If we are talking about equality between the policeman and the criminal, we are on dangerous ground.
>
> I would remind this Court that we are not talking about the police versus the defendant. We are talking about the people versus the defendant. In the same way that we would not talk about the Army or the Marine Corps versus the Viet Cong, but we would talk about the United States versus the Viet Cong.
>
> If this is to be our objective, to limit the use of the confession in criminal cases, then you are taking from the police a most important piece of evidence in every case that they bring before a court of justice.
>
> Police officers are public servants. They are not attempting to put innocent people in jail.
>
> They want to follow the dictates of this Court, and they will follow them to the best of their ability, but they, too, are human beings. They do have, however, experience and knowledge, which many of us lack, because this is their job, investigation of crime, and we have not, as lawyers, paid attention to their jobs.
>
> We have seldom been down to the police station and asked, "What can we do to assist you in your problems?"

The Supreme Court of the United States was split on the issue. In a six-to-three majority decision, the Court held that the right to counsel started at the interrogation stage. Chief Justice Warren who delivered the judgment of the majority felt that if the guarantee in the Fifth Amendment of the Constitution which protects a person from being "compelled in any criminal case to be a witness against himself" was to have any meaning, then it had to apply at the interrogation stage. Without a lawyer to advise him of his rights, where he wanted one, that right was meaningless. He expressed it this way:

> Today, then, there can be no doubt that the Fifth Amendment privilege is available outside of criminal court proceedings and serves to protect persons in all settings in which their freedom of action is curtailed from being compelled to incriminate themselves. We have concluded that without proper safeguards the process of an in-custody interrogation of persons suspected or accused of crime contains inherently compelling pressures which work to undermine the individual's will to resist and to compel him to speak where he would not otherwise do so freely. In order to combat these pressures and to permit a full opportunity to exercise the privilege against self-incrimination, the accused must be adequately and effectively apprised of his rights and the exercise of those rights must be fully honoured.

What were those "compelling pressures"? He explained those earlier in his judgment:

> An individual swept from familiar surroundings into police custody, surrounded by antagonistic forces, and subjected to the techniques of persuasion described above cannot be otherwise than under compulsion to speak. As a practical matter, the compulsion to speak in the isolated setting of the police station may well be greater than in courts or other official investigations, where there are often impartial observers to guard against intimidation or trickery.

Chief Justice Warren recognized that because the "circumstances surrounding in-custody interrogation can operate very quickly to overbear the will of one merely made aware of his privilege by his interrogators", the accused should have counsel present at the interrogation to ensure that the Fifth Amendment privilege is protected. There were additional reasons why counsel should be present:

> If the accused decides to talk to his interrogators, the assistance of counsel can mitigate the dangers of untrustworthiness. With a lawyer present the likelihood that the police will practise coercion is reduced, and if coercion is nevertheless exercised the lawyer can testify to it in court. The presence of a lawyer can also help guarantee that the accused gives a fully accurate statement to the police and that the statement is rightly reported by the prosecution at trial.

The Court concluded that an individual held for interrogation had to be clearly informed that he had the right to consult with a lawyer and to have the lawyer with him during the interrogation. What happened if he could not afford the services of a lawyer? Was the state required to provide a lawyer for a person who could not afford one? Chief Justice Warren recognized that most people who appeared before the criminal courts were generally the poor and underprivileged. If the protections listed in the Bill of Rights were to apply to everyone, then there was an obligation upon the state not to take advantage of them. He recognized that the state is not required to relieve an accused of his poverty. On the other hand, "they have the obligation not to take advantage of indigence in the administration of justice."

If every citizen was to be given equal protection under the Bill of Rights, then everyone should have equal opportunity to exercise those rights. This meant that if a person could not afford to hire a lawyer, there was an obligation upon the state to provide him with one. So that an accused could fully understand his rights, it was necessary for the police to advise him that not only did he have the right to consult with an attorney but that if he was indigent, a lawyer would be appointed to represent him. This additional warning was necessary because most people believed that they had the right to counsel only if they already retained a lawyer or possessed the funds to hire one. Therefore, an accused had to be effectively and expressly told that a lawyer would be appointed if he could not afford one.

Another question which faced the court in Miranda was whether an accused, once he agreed to answer questions, could request the interrogator to stop at any time. Chief Justice Warren was of the view that he could:

> Without the right to cut off questioning, the setting of in-custody interrogation operates on the individual to overcome free choice producing a statement after the privilege has been once invoked. If the individual states that he wants an attorney, the interrogation must cease until an attorney is present. At that time, the individual must have an opportunity to confer with the attorney and to have him present during any subsequent questioning. If the individual cannot obtain an attorney and indicates that he wants one before speaking to the police, they must respect his decision to remain silent.

But he was prepared to accept that an accused could waive all of these rights once they were fully explained to him. The silence of an accused, however, did not mean that he intended to waive his rights. The accused's waiver had to be a free and voluntary one, based upon his knowledge of his rights and his express desire to forego those rights. Nothing less should be accepted by the courts.

Mr. Justice Harlan who expressed the dissenting view of the Court was concerned that these protections would seriously hamper effective police investigation:

> What the Court largely ignores is that its rules impair, if they will not eventually serve wholly to frustrate, an instrument of law enforcement that has long and quite reasonably been thought worth the price paid for it. There can be little doubt that the Court's new code would markedly decrease the number of confessions. To warn the suspect that he may remain silent and remind him that his confession may be used in court are minor obstructions. To require also an express waiver by an accused and an end to questioning whenever he demurs must heavily handicap questioning. And to suggest or provide counsel for the suspect simply invites the end of the interrogation.
>
> How much harm this decision will inflict on law enforcement cannot fairly be predicted with accuracy. . . . We do know that some crimes cannot be solved without confessions, that ample expert testimony attests to their importance in crime control,

and that the Court is taking a real risk with society's welfare in imposing its new regime on the country. The social costs of crime are too great to call the new rules anything but a hazardous experimentation.

# Right To Counsel In Canada

The leaders of the five provinces, still closely connected to Great Britain, did not feel that it was necessary to enshrine any fundamental rights in a Bill of Rights or a Charter of Rights at the time of Confederation in 1867. It was believed that our rights and freedoms could be best protected through the instrument of parliamentary democracy. But after the Second World War, there developed a view, particularly with the increased intervention of government into the daily lives of private citizens, that Canada should have its own Bill of Rights. In 1960, a Bill of Rights was passed by the Parliament of Canada applicable only to federal legislation. Unfortunately, the language was couched in negative terms (. . . no law of Canada shall be construed or applied so as to deprive a person . . .). The result was that it soon became only an instrument which the courts used to interpret statutes. It gave the courts little power to strike down legislation which infringed the rights enumerated. It contained no procedure to remedy where there was a breach. It was necessary to wait an additional 22 years for the Charter of Rights and Freedoms to be passed. The right to "retain and instruct counsel without delay" enacted in section 2(*c*)(ii) of the Bill of Rights, 1960 was now repeated in the Charter in positive terms. There was also a new right added: The right on arrest or detention "to be informed of . . ." the right to counsel. The words used in section 10(*b*) are as follows:

10. Everyone has the right on arrest or detention

    (*b*) to retain and instruct counsel without delay and to be informed of that right.

Until the Bill of Rights, 1960, Canada had followed the English tradition with respect to the right to counsel. If a person was to be granted the right to counsel, then that right was no more than "the right to be represented at trial by counsel." Although the right to counsel at the interrogation stage was not recognized in the United States until *Escobedo v. Illinois*, 1964 and fully developed in *Miranda v. Arizona* in 1966, Canada at least recognized the right to counsel at that stage in the Bill of Rights of 1960, notwithstanding the unfortunate wording of the legislation.

Between 1960 and 1982, there were some attempts to extend that right beyond the interrogation stage but they were only partially successful. For example, in *Regina v. Brownridge*, Brownridge had asked to consult with his lawyer after a demand had been made upon him to supply a sample of his breath to be tested in a breathalyzer. When the police officer refused, Brownridge also refused to provide the sample and was charged with the offence of refusing to comply with a breathalyzer demand. Mr. Justice Laskin, who later became Chief Justice of Canada, wrote,

> [I]t does not lie with an arresting police officer to determine in his discretion or on a superior's instructions whether or when to permit an arrested person to contact his counsel. The right to retain and instruct counsel without delay can only have meaning to an arrested or detained person if it is taken as raising a correlative obligation upon the police authorities to facilitate contact with counsel. This means allowing him upon his request to use the telephone for that purpose if one is available.

Subsequent decisions of the courts attempted to expand this right by saying that once an accused asked to talk to his lawyer, the police had an obligation to provide him with some privacy whether he spoke to him personally or by telephone. Most of the cases dealing with this issue, however, mainly centred around drinking and driving offences. At best, denial of the right to counsel only gave the accused the right to assert that he had a reasonable excuse to refuse to comply with a breathalyzer demand. None of the authorities was prepared to go as far as the Supreme Court of the United States in Escobedo or Miranda in imposing an obligation upon the police to inform the accused of his right to consult with counsel. That right has now been guaranteed by section 10(*b*) of the Charter.

It is only in rare instances that a Constitution can provide a comprehensive definition of the rights and freedoms it seeks to guarantee. A constitution is only a skeleton; it is up to the courts to add the flesh necessary to satisfy the needs of society and the sinew strong enough to withstand its criticism.

The Americans have had their Bill of Rights for over 200 years; the Charter of Rights and Freedoms is just a little over 3 years old. Canadian courts are only now beginning to test the waters of this new Charter. Only now are some of the cases wending their way through the trial courts, past the provincial appellate courts, and on their way to the Supreme Court of Canada. How are the present judicial opinions developing?

In dealing with the right to counsel, obviously the first question is when do the rights of a person arise? The section says "on arrest or detention." The word "arrest" has been considered and interpreted by the courts for over five centuries. Although there have been many conflicting decisions, it is now generally settled that any form of physical restraint is an arrest. In other words, when a police officer says to a citizen, "you are under arrest," those words alone will not necessarily constitute an arrest. There must be some form of actual restraint of the person, usually by touching him. But it is not necessary that there always be some touching of the person or physical contact; a person may be under arrest if the words used by the officer clearly indicate to him that if he attempts to leave, he will be physically restrained and the person does in fact submit to his loss of liberty.

It is generally accepted that when a legislative body such as Parliament passes a law, each word that it uses is intended to have a specific meaning. "Detention," therefore, must have a different meaning from "arrest." If arrest is the highest form of physical restraint exercised by a police officer, then detention must mean something less. What can it mean?

In 1980, the Supreme Court of Canada was asked to interpret the meaning of "detention" in *Regina v. Chromiak.* In that case Kenneth Chromiak was driving his motor vehicle when he was stopped by a police officer because of his erratic driving. As the officer approached the vehicle Chromiak stepped out of it and staggered slightly. His breath also smelled of alcohol. The officer asked him to perform certain sobriety tests which he did. Based on those tests the officer formed the belief that he might be impaired and asked him to provide a breath sample into a roadside approved testing device. Chromiak, however, refused and said that he wanted his lawyer present before he would do so. He was charged with refusing to provide a breath sample for the roadside tester.

The Bill of Rights, 1960 stated that "no law of Canada shall be construed or applied so as to deprive a person . . . who has been arrested or detained . . . of the right to retain and instruct counsel without delay. . . ." His lawyer argued before the Supreme Court of Canada that Chromiak was entitled to speak to his lawyer before he gave a breath sample because he was "detained" by a police officer. The Supreme Court of Canada was obviously in a dilemma. If it found that a "detention" occurred when the police officer stopped Mr. Chromiak, it would mean that any time a motorist was suspected of having alcohol in his system and an officer wanted to obtain a breath sample for the roadside screening device (which does not determine the amount of alcohol in his system but only if there is enough to warrant a test by a breathalyzer machine), a police officer would have to drive a motorist to the nearest telephone so that he could try to contact his lawyer. It would be time consuming and possibly render the whole roadside screening system useless. On the other hand, any other interpretation would ignore the word's ordinary meaning — restraint of liberty. If the motorist had ignored the police officer's demand, there is little doubt that he would have been restrained of his liberty. Thus in order to prevent a frustration of the use of the roadside screening device, the Supreme Court of Canada was compelled to conclude that "detain" meant being held in custody.

With the enactment of the Charter of Rights and Freedoms, the question came up again. This time most courts decided that the matter had been settled by the Chromiak case: a person who was stopped by a police officer and requested by him not only to supply a breath sample for a roadside screening device, but also to accompany the officer to the police station to provide a sample for a breathalyzer was not "detained" and therefore need not be told of his right to counsel nor entitled to consult with one. However, the Saskatchewan Court of Appeal came to a different conclusion. In *Regina v. Therens*, Mr. Justice Tallis felt that because the Charter of Rights and Freedoms is a constitutional document and the supreme law of Canada, it had to be given a place of particular importance. It had not been passed for the benefit of judges, lawyers or law professors. It was enacted for the ordinary citizen. If it was to have any meaning for the ordinary citizen, then it should be interpreted in such a way that the ordinary citizen could understand it. He expressed that view in these words:

> Our nation's constitutional ideals have been enshrined in the Charter and it will not be a "living" charter unless it is interpreted in a meaningful way from the standpoint of an average citizen who seldom has a brush with the law. The fundamental rights accorded to a citizen under s. 10(*b*) should be approached on the basis of giving the word "detention" its popular interpretation, in other words its natural or ordinary meaning. The implementation and application of the Charter should not be blunted or thwarted by technical or legalistic interpretations of ordinary words of the English language. Using this approach, our citizens will not be placed in a position of feeling that the statements in the Charter are only rights in theory. If these rights are to survive and be available on a day-to-day basis we must resist the temptation to opt in favour of a restrictive approach. If a restrictive approach is adopted in defining the word "detain" then this will be tantamount to saying that the law does not recognize rights under s. 10(*b*) as applying to an accused before arrest.

Paul Therens had been asked to accompany an officer to a police station to provide a breath sample for a breathalyzer. It was conceded by the Crown that if he had refused to go along with the officer he would have been arrested and placed in custody. The ordinary citizen in that situation would expect that he would be subjected to some force if he did not comply with the officer's demand. And so the Court concluded that any form of restraint, even though temporary, was a detention.

On May 23, 1985, the controversy was finally settled by the Supreme Court of Canada who agreed with that interpretation of section 10(*b*). Mr. Justice LeDain delivering the majority judgment of the Court, rejected the suggestion that the Court was required to give the same meaning to the word "detention" under the Bill of Rights. In his view, the Court could not,

> avoid bearing in mind an evident fact of Canadian judicial history, which must be squarely and frankly faced: that on the whole, with some notable exceptions, the courts have felt some uncertainty or ambivalence in the application of the *Canadian Bill of Rights* because it did not reflect a clear constitutional mandate to make judicial decisions having the effect of limiting or qualifying the traditional sovereignty of Parliament.

He noted that section 1 of the Charter entitles the Court to impose upon a guarantee "such reasonable limits as are demonstrably justified in a free and democratic society." That very term entitles the Court to interpret a right or guarantee in a more flexible way than under the Bill of Rights, which had no limiting provision. As far as he was concerned, a different approach had to be taken in interpreting the Charter of Rights and Freedoms.

He then turned to an examination of the purpose of section 10. This was how Chief Justice Dickson had approached the question in assessing the reasonableness or unreasonableness of the impact of a search or of a statute authorizing a search in *Hunter v. Southam Inc.* One had to, in the words of Chief Justice Dickson, "delineate the nature of the interests it is meant to protect." Mr. Justice LeDain found that the purpose of section 10 of the Charter was to,

> ensure that in certain situations a person is made aware of the right to counsel and is permitted to retain and instruct counsel without delay. The situations specified by s. 10 — arrest and detention — are obviously not the only ones in which a person may reasonably require the assistance of counsel, but they are situations in which the restraint of liberty might otherwise effectively prevent access to counsel or induce a person to assume that he or she is unable to retain and instruct counsel. In its use of the word "detention", s. 10 of the Charter is directed to a restraint of liberty other than arrest in which a person may reasonably require the assistance of counsel but might be prevented or impeded from retaining and instructing counsel without delay but for the constitutional guarantee.

He next turned to a consideration of the meaning and extent of "detention." The courts had always held that detention meant a deprivation of liberty by physical constraint. But what about the situation where a police officer or other agent of the state assumes control over the movement of a person by a demand or direction which may have significant legal consequences and which prevents or impedes access to counsel? In other words, should the courts restrict detention to a compulsion of a physical nature, as courts have always done in the past, or should it be extended to compulsion of a psychological or mental nature which inhibited the will as effectively as the application, or threat of application, of physical force. Previous decisions presumed that a person who was the subject of a demand or direction by a police officer or other agent of the state could reasonably regard himself as free to refuse to comply.

Mr. Justice LeDain rejected those earlier cases. As far as he was concerned,

> ... it is not realistic, as a general rule, to regard compliance with a demand or direction by a police officer as truly voluntary, in the sense that the citizen feels that he or she has the choice to obey or not, even where there is in fact a lack of statutory or common law authority for the demand or direction and therefore an absence of criminal liability for failure to comply with it. Most citizens are not aware of the precise limits of police authority. Rather than risk the application of physical force or prosecution for wilful obstruction, the reasonable person is likely to err on the side of caution, assume lawful authority and comply with the demand. The element of psychological compulsion, in the form of a reasonable perception of suspension of freedom of choice, is enough to make the restraint of liberty involuntary. Detention may be effected without the appli-

cation or threat of application of physical restraint if the person concerned submits or acquiesces in the deprivation of liberty and reasonably believes the choice to do otherwise does not exist.

But that did not end the matter. He now had to consider the effect of section 1 of the Charter. Section 1 recognizes that there can be reasonable limits to the rights and freedoms enumerated. Those reasonable limits must be such as can be "demonstrably justified in a free and democratic society." He noted that the breathalyzer provisions do not expressly purport to limit the right to counsel; if there is to be any limit, it had to be by way of implication from their terms or operating requirements.

Sections 234 and 236 of the Criminal Code permit the use of a breathalyzer test as evidence provided that the test is taken not later than two hours after the time when the offence is alleged to have been committed. These sections must be distinguished from section 234.1, that is, where a demand is made to provide a sample for a roadside screening device. The section requires that the sample must be provided "forthwith." There is no two-hour leeway period which would give a motorist a reasonable opportunity to consult with his counsel.

Mr. Justice LeDain felt that a two-hour leeway period did not make it impractical for police officers to carry out their duty to enforce Canada's drinking and driving laws and still respect the right to counsel. It was a different matter where there was a requirement, as in section 234.1, to provide a sample for a roadside screening device "forthwith." This distinction had been pointed out by the Saskatchewan Court of Appeal in *Regina v. Talbourdet* decided on March 1, 1984. There the Saskatchewan Court of Appeal decided that section 1 of the Charter did import a reasonable limitation on the right to counsel. The Court concluded that:

> For perfectly obvious reasons it is a crime in Canada and elsewhere to drive a motor vehicle while one's ability to do so is impaired by alcohol. And everyone whose blood-alcohol level exceeds 80 mg of alcohol in 100 ml of blood is now reasonably regarded by the criminal law of Canada to be thus impaired. To provide for the effective enforcement of this law, Parliament has justifiably empowered Canada's peace officers, whenever they have "reasonable and probable grounds" to believe that a person is breaking the law, to demand of that person that he or she submit to a breathalyzer test. But often a person's blood-alcohol level will exceed the legal limit without that fact being obvious. A peace officer may well suspect a person of committing an offence — there may be a distinct odour of alcohol — but, having regard for the fact that ours is a free society, the law requires that there be more than mere "suspicion" before a police officer can require a person to submit to a breathalyzer test; he has to have "reasonable and probable grounds" to do so.
>
> And this, of course, is where the roadside screening device comes into the picture. It is an investigative tool. Its purpose is to resolve the doubt which will often exist between "suspicion" on the one hand and "reasonable and probable ground" on the other. When a policeman finds himself in that grey area between suspecting that an offence of this kind is being committed, and having reasonable and probable grounds for believing it is being committed, he may, providing there is good reason for his suspicion, ask the

driver to clarify the position by submitting to a preliminary test conducted by means of a roadside screening device. This is a minor inconvenience and the person upon whom such a demand for clarification has been made runs no risk of being found guilty of any offence by submitting to the test. If he passes the test then he is free to go on his way; if he fails it then, of course, there are reasonable and probable grounds to believe that he may be guilty of an offence, and, in that event, a peace officer may make a further demand of him, namely that he submit to a more definitive test by means of a breathalyzer machine. And at that stage he has the right to consult a lawyer.

Another question which will have to be considered is what the police must do so as to inform a person of his right to retain and instruct counsel. Must he explain that right in specific and clear words or is it enough that there be a sign on the wall which the accused can see or to which the officer points? At one extreme is the decision of the Prince Edward Island Court of Appeal in *Regina v. Ahern* where it was felt that it was enough if there was a sign on the wall capable of being read by the accused. However, it is doubtful whether this approach is one which will be accepted by other courts in view of the importance placed upon the right to counsel. It is generally recognized that there is a duty upon the police officer to explain the right to counsel in clear and unambiguous words.

But is the police officer required to do anything more, such as ask the accused if he understands that right or even assist him to telephone counsel? Some people, particularly if this is their first brush with the law, may find the police station an overwhelming and frightening place. It may also be frightening and oppressive to young people, or the elderly or those who have some mental or physical infirmity. Is there a duty upon the police officer in these instances to assist the individual in exercising his rights?

Here the courts have moved carefully in attempting to arrive at a solution that can satisfy both the rights of the individual and the need for effective law enforcement. Upon whom should lie the responsibility for deciding if the accused understands about his right to counsel? Is that obligation upon the police or is it upon the accused to establish that he did not understand what he was told by the police? In *Regina v. Anderson*, the Ontario Court of Appeal concluded that the primary obligation had to be upon the accused. Mr. Justice Tarnopolsky, delivering the judgment of the Court, was of the view that,

> absent proof of circumstances indicating that the accused did not understand his right to retain counsel when he was informed of it, the onus has to be on him to prove that he asked for the right but it was denied or he was denied any opportunity to even ask for it.

The final question that must be considered is what happens when the accused asserts his right to counsel? Are the police entitled to continue to question him or must they stop immediately and give him the opportunity to talk to his lawyer? If a person is told that he has a right to counsel and says that he wants to talk to one, are the police still entitled to go ahead and interrogate him? Must they stop and let him speak to the lawyer before they can ask him any questions? If he does not ask to see a lawyer but merely says that he will not answer questions, can the police continue to question him?

All of those issues were considered by the Ontario Court of Appeal in *Regina v. Manninen*. Ronald Manninen was arrested two days after a robbery had been committed and he was told of the reasons for his arrest and of his right to counsel. He was also cautioned to which he replied, "Prove it, I ain't saying anything until I see my lawyer. I want to see my lawyer." One of the officers, however, proceeded to question him. He was asked his name and address and answered the questions. He was then asked:

> Q. Where is the knife that you had along with this (showing him a $Co_2$ gun found in the car) when you ripped off the Mac's Milk on Wilson Avenue?
> A. He's lying. When I was in the store I only had the gun. The knife was in the tool box in the car.

Based on this response, he was convicted at his trial. The Ontario Court of Appeal, however, decided that the trial judge should not have admitted the statement into evidence or considered it in reaching his verdict. Associate Chief Justice MacKinnon, who delivered the judgment of the Court, gave these reasons:

> Immediately after the appellant's clear assertion of his right to remain silent and his desire to consult his lawyer, the constable commenced his questioning. The first two questions might be described as "innocuous" in the circumstances of this case, being a request for the appellant's name and address. The third question was in a completely different category. "Where is the knife that you had along with this (showing the $Co_2$ gun) when you ripped off the Mac's Milk on Wilson Avenue?" was based on a presumption of guilt and the answer was devastating to the defence. The presumption of innocence under s. 11(*d*) of the Charter was certainly of no assistance to the accused at this stage. More importantly, the question was asked as if the appellant had expressed no desire to remain silent and to see his lawyer.

He also took pains to stress that once an accused asserted his right to consult with his lawyer before he said anything, that right had to be respected. If the officer continued to question the accused and ignored that right then any answer given should not be admitted in evidence. The fact that the questions were answered by Manninen did not mean that he intended to waive his right to counsel. The Court recognized that if Manninen had spoken to his lawyer, he would probably have been told to keep quiet. Nevertheless, the Court considered that an accused's right to counsel was such an important guarantee under the Charter that if breached, any evidence obtained as a consequence should not be considered by the court.

Eventually, issues such as those raised by *Manninen* and *Anderson* will be considered by the Supreme Court of Canada. That Court will, it is hoped, give a definitive but probably not final answer as to the scope of the right to counsel under the Charter. Until that day, the lower courts must grope with this issue in an effort to strike a balance between the fundamental freedoms of everyone and the rights of society as a whole to be protected from those who are prepared to break society's laws.

# 11

# Remedying The Breach

For what is done to any one may be done to everyone; besides, being all members of one body, that is, of the English Commonwealth, one man should not suffer wrongfully, but all should be sensible, and endeavour his preservation; otherwise they give way an inlet of the sea of will and power, upon their laws and liberties, which are the boundaries to keep out tyranny and oppression; and who assists not in such cases, betrays his own rights, and is overrun, and of a free man made a slave when he thinks not of it, or regards it not, and so shunning the censure of turbulency, incurs the guilt of treachery to the present and future generations.

John Lilburne

Decency, security, and liberty alike demand that government officials shall be subjected to the same rules of conduct that are commands to the citizens. In a government of laws, existence of the government will be imperilled if it fails to observe the law scrupulously. Our government is the potent, omnipresent teacher. For good or for ill, it teaches the whole people by its example. Crime is contagious. If the government becomes a law-breaker, it breeds contempt for law; it invites anarchy. To declare that in the administration of the criminal law the end justifies the means — to declare that the government may commit crimes in order to secure the conviction of a private criminal — would bring terrible retribution. Against that pernicious doctrine the court should resolutely set its face.

Mr. Justice Brandeis, dissenting,<br>*Olmstead v. United States* (1928)

ROPER: Arrest him.
ALICE: Yes!
MORE: For what?
ALICE: He's dangerous!
ROPER: For libel; he's a spy.
ALICE: He is! Arrest him!
MARGARET: Father, that man's bad.
MORE: There is no law against that.
ROPER: There is! God's law!
MORE: Then God can arrest him.
ROPER: Sophistication upon sophistication!
MORE: No, sheer simplicity. The law, Roper, the law. I know what's legal not what's right. And I'll stick to what's legal.

ROPER: Then you set Man's law above God's!

MORE: No far below; but let me draw your attention to a fact — I'm not God. The currents and eddies of right and wrong, which you find such plain-sailing, I can't navigate, I'm no voyager. But in the thickets of the law, Oh there I'm a forester. I doubt if there's a man alive who could follow me there, thank God. . .

ALICE: While you talk, he's gone.

MORE: And go he should if he was the devil himself until he broke the law!

ROPER: So now you'd give the Devil benefit of law!

MORE: Yes. What would you do? Cut a great road through the law to get after the Devil?

ROPER: I'd cut down every law in England to do that!

MORE: And when the last law was down, and the Devil turned round on you — where would you hide, Roper, the laws all being flat? This country's planted thick with laws from coast to coast — Man's laws, not God's — and if you cut them down — and you're just the man to do it — d'you really think you could stand upright in the winds that would blow then? Yes, I'd give the Devil benefit of law, for my own safety's sake.

Robert Bolt, A Man for All Seasons

. . . the criminal is to go free because the constable has blundered. . .

Mr. Justice Benjamin Cardozo, dissenting,<br>*People v. Defore*, 1926

Donald Comrie was 20 years of age and lived at home with his parents in the family farm house just north of the village of King. During the week he was employed at National Cash Register in Peterborough. But on the weekends, to earn a little extra money, he worked at Knoll's Service Station which is three and one half miles east of Peterborough on Highway 7.

On Saturday March 23, 1968, Henry Knoll, the owner of the service station, had gone into Peterborough for a haircut and left the station in charge of Donald. Henry's 13-year-old nephew, John Frisch was visiting and was helping Donald change a licence plate. At precisely five to twelve, Henry Knoll returned from Peterborough carrying his groceries and joked with John and Donald before going into his home, which was next door to the station, to put the groceries away.

Henry had two watch dogs, a Doberman Pincher which he chained behind the candy counter inside the station and a German Shepherd which he permitted to run free. While they were working, Donald and John noticed that the dogs began to growl. John offered to go and see what was the matter but Donald said he would go because he was closer. He was away only a few minutes when John heard a sound which he described as a "crack." Immediately the growling stopped and everything became very silent.

The sudden silence aroused John's curiosity; he decided to go into the office to see what was going on. As he got inside, he saw the back of someone running away from the station towards the highway carrying a rifle in his right hand. The man was wearing a red hunting cap and khaki coloured jacket.

John could not see Donald anywhere around and so he called him three or four times. Finally he heard a groan and found him lying on the floor behind the counter. He immediately ran to get his uncle who followed him back quickly to the office. When they arrived, Henry's wife was already there wiping Donald's face. Henry tried to take his pulse but could not get one. The police were immediately called and arrived within fifteen minutes. John thought the man was about six feet tall, of medium build and had dark hair. He told this to Constable Kenneth McDermid of the Ontario Provincial Police who was called to the scene.

A search was conducted of the office and in particular the cash register. Fifty-five dollars in bills was missing. Henry Knoll was sure of this because he had checked the register that morning. A search was also conducted of the area for the assailant. The only trace was a brass cartridge case for a 44-40 calibre rifle and the footprints of a man on the shoulder of the road.

Approximately two months later on June 2 Inspector John Lidstone of the Ontario Provincial Police arrived at the residence of Gordon Wray in Peterborough, Ontario. He was looking for a Winchester 44-40, 1892 model rifle which he understood belonged to Gordon Wray's youngest son James. Gordon Wray and his wife invited Inspector Lidstone into the house and gave him permission to look around. Inspector Lidstone went through the house but couldn't find the rifle he was looking for. James Wray had a number of other rifles some of which he kept in his own bedroom and others in his parents' bedroom. The rifle which Inspector Lidstone was trying to find had been last seen on March 22 when Gorden Wray had shown it to his brother who was visiting him for the weekend.

At 3:00 o'clock that afternoon Inspector Lidstone spoke to John Wray, an older brother of James Wray. John lived in Toronto where he worked as a commissioned salesman. He usually came home each weekend. Inspector Lidstone asked John if he could search his car and John readily agreed. The Inspector told him that he was investigating the Donald Comrie murder and was looking for the missing rifle. John replied that he knew that he was. Inspector Lidstone then asked John if his brother James had been using his car on March 23. John told him that no one had been using his car that day.

Two days later on June 4, Inspector Lidstone returned again to the Wray home and saw John washing his car in front of his house. He asked

John if he would come along to the O.P.P. station to discuss his activities on March 23. John said he would. Inspector Lidstone was aware that John was having financial problems because John's room-mate in Toronto had not paid his share of the rent. He asked John if he would take a polygraph test and John agreed because, "I have nothing to hide." Inspector Lidstone had already arranged with a private detective, John Jurems of Toronto, that he might be bringing somebody for a test.

In 1968, few Canadians knew anything about the polygraph or lie detector test and even fewer had any training in the use of one. John Jurems had taken his training in the United States and was one of few people in Canada who professed to have any expertise in the field. He claimed to have given over 5,000 tests in 13 years as a private investigator.

When John Wray was taken to Jurems' office in Toronto, he was never told that he was not required to take the lie detector test nor was he told that he would be first questioned by Jurems and his conversation overheard by Inspector Lidstone and taped. John Wray asked Jurems if the results of the examination would be used against him and was told "not necessarily."

Although the test itself only took thirty-eight and one half minutes, John was interrogated by John Jurems for almost five hours. The police were anxious to find out if John Wray knew where the rifle was. Jurems knew that if he was going to get that information from him, he had to create an atmosphere in the interrogation room which would condition John to give that information. To do so, he told him a series of lies about the evidence in the possession of the police and which he said incriminated him. How he did this was to ask him questions in such a way that the only answer that John Wray could give would be "yes".

After interrogating him for an hour and a half in this fashion, Jurems left the room and Inspector Lidstone and another officer entered. They questioned John Wray about a trip down the highway past the service station at about 11:30 p.m. on the day of the shooting. After a half hour of questioning by the officers, they left the room and Jurems returned and continued his interrogation. An hour and a half later, Jurems again left the room and the police officers returned. This time they questioned him for an hour and a half. They accused him directly of being involved in the murder of Donald Comrie but John Wray continued to deny it. The interrogation went this way,

LIDSTONE: He just happened to be there. He just happened to be there, didn't he? He was shot when you happened to be down there with your car, the car that was seen leaving. The loaded gun, the shells missing from the house. The gun, the case, of course the case was necessary. You had to pass some of the neighbours. In case any of the neighbours looked out and saw you with a rifle get in the car that morning. They would say, oh, ho, there's something wrong here. But you walk out with a case and nobody pays any attention, so then the case. It just happens that you're down there, down in that same area at the same time then back to the garage. You would have an alibi . . . You're sitting there sweating . . . chills . . . I recognize the signs of stress and you're under stress.

John Jurems decided that it was an appropriate time to enter the room.

JUREMS: Could I talk to John for a few minutes here. There's something I thought of . . .

JUREMS: John, now listen to me good. Now I was through the war, see, and I've been around. Now remember this and remember it good. Have you ever seen rubby dubbies, winos?

WRAY: Yes.

JUREMS: Have you ever seen the alcoholics?

WRAY: Yes.

JUREMS: Do you know why they go that way. Have you got a clue?

WRAY: No. I have an idea.

JUREMS: I'll explain you something. You have the cerebreal, cerebreal and then you have the tholmus and the hipatholmus. Now, a person is going to blot out something he doesn't like, see, but you can't do it, John. You just no can do, because the subconscious mind takes over and you never live it down. Every time you want to do something you think of it. Now here's this poor joker, he's in the grave, oh, yes, now you can never go to him and explain to him, say I'm sorry I did it. He won't understand you. Do you believe in E.S.P., Extra Sensory Perception?

WRAY: I don't understand it too much, but I know it exists.

JUREMS: All right. All right, do you know what happens when they're dead. The spirit takes off.

WRAY: Yes.

JUREMS: The body's spirit takes off. Now his body's lying there in the grave. Now for Christ sake, John, if you did it, see, if you did it and if you think for one goddamn minute you can live with this all your life without telling you'll never make it. It will haunt you and in about five years time you will be in the goddamn with the rubby dubs trying to hide it, you'll be trying to get in behind some curtains, you'll be trying to pull a shroud around you but you'll never make it, see. You get half a dozen of those rubby dubs and you bring them in here and I'll put them on the machine and they tell me why they're like that. You know why? They're trying to forget something they did that was very goddamn serious, very bad, see, but they never make it. They go rubby dub, they go here, they steal here, they do every goddamn thing wrong, all their life eh. Now, if you committed this goddamn thing, see, tell them, tell the cops. What the hell can you get? They're not going to hang you. That's out. But at least you've got it and after that you can live with your conscience. But how the hell are you going to go to the grave and explain? You can't, and if you think for one minute, John, remember this that that boy has relatives, that boy has a mother and brothers and sisters and do you know what a vindictive person is? Eh? They'll go for you and maybe a year, maybe five years from now you'll be going down the road and some son of a bitch will run you off the road. You'll never know why, but you'll guess why. See. Now you were there, see. You were in the goddamn service station. Now when I asked you whether it was an accident you said, yes, and it was an accident, see. There's extenuating circumstances because a person goes in there you didn't go in — you don't go in the — there to shoot the fellow. When a fellow goes in there, sure, what happened to this — look at that goofy one that came here from Montreal, he shot three people in a bank robbery, what did he get, he's out now. He didn't even serve ten years. Three people in a bank robbery. See. So you went in there. You didn't go in there to shoot the guy, but the gun went off. It was at close range. What did he do, grab the gun from you. Did he grab the rifle from you? Eh?

WRAY: No.

JUREMS: What happened? Well, get it off your chest, man, you're young, but in a few years you'll be out. But if you think that you're going to live with this, laddie, you'll never ever never make it. It's going to bug you for the rest of your goddamn life. And you try and sleep, that's the sticker, you try and lay down and go to sleep. Now what the hell happened there. Did you get in a tussle with him — what happened. Well, spit it out. Your mother knows, your brother knows, your sisters, know, your uncle knows. Do you think you can kid your mother for one minute — never! Your mother knows. That's why she tried to protect you. You know. Now what the hell happened, eh? will you tell us what happened.

WRAY: Yes.

JUREMS: Okay, tell us what happened.

WRAY: I went in. . .

JUREMS: You went in, talk a little louder, John.

WRAY: I went in there.

JUREMS: Yeah.

WRAY: To Knolls'.

JUREMS: Yes, you went in to Knoll's yeah.

WRAY: And the boy —

JUREMS: Which boy?

WRAY: There's only one boy.

JUREMS: Just the boy that was shot. Yeah, what happened:

WRAY: He came out.

JUREMS: Talk a little louder, John.

WRAY: He came out.

WRAY: And asked me what I wanted.

JUREMS: He asked you what you wanted.

WRAY: And I told him to open the till.

JUREMS: And told him to open the till. Was it closed?

WRAY: Yes.

JUREMS: And what did he say?

WRAY: He said, all right.

JUREMS: He opened the till, yeah.

WRAY: And then he — he gave me the money.

JUREMS: He gave you the money. Well, what the hell did you shoot him for?

WRAY: It was an accident.

JUREMS: It was an accident. Sure, you showed it on your check it was an accident. All the reactions you gave me when I asked you was the shooting an accident, you said, yes, and it's an accident. Well, what the hell is wrong with that. All they are going to charge you with. You went in there, your intentions weren't to do any harm to the man. Where is the gun now?

WRAY: I don't know exactly.

JUREMS: Well, where did you drop it, on the way home?

WRAY: No, eh?

JUREMS: On the way to Toronto?

WRAY: Yes.

JUREMS: Around Oshawa:

WRAY: No.

JUREMS: Where?

WRAY: Near Omemee someplace.
JUREMS: Where?
WRAY: Omemee.
JUREMS: Omemee, in the ditch?
WRAY: No.
JUREMS: Where?
WRAY: In the swamp.
JUREMS: In the swamp. Could you, could you show the police where it is?
WRAY: Yes.
JUREMS: Now you're talking like a man. Jesus Christ, John, because you got to live with it all your life, man, oh, man, you'll never make it if you a person sleeps, hasn't it been bothering you?
WRAY: Yes.
JUREMS: Have you been sleeping well?
WRAY: Yes, fairly well.
JUREMS: But it bothers you. A person never lives it down. Now when, now I'll call in the — the Inspector there and you can tell him what happened, okay. Will you tell him?
WRAY: Yes

Inspector Lidstone suddenly entered the room and told John Wray that he was charged with the murder of Donald Comrie. He asked John Wray if he would show him where the rifle had been abandoned and John agreed to do so. Inspector Lidstone called his office and discovered that a lawyer had been retained by Wray's father to represent him and wanted to speak to John. Inspector Lidstone was concerned that if he allowed the lawyer to speak to John Wray he would advise him not to cooperate with the police and show them the location. And so he did not call him back. Within a few minutes the two officers and John Wray left Jurems' office and drove back to Peterborough where they went to a swamp located off Fyfe Bay Road. There they searched for the rifle without success. The next morning, the search was continued and this time a rifle and a red hunting cap were found. The rifle was sent off to the Centre of Forensic Science in Toronto. There tests conducted on the rifle established that it had fired the bullet that had killed Donald Comrie.

Mr. Justice Henderson who presided over the trial had no hesitation in excluding the confession because it had been obtained as a result of inducements offered by Jurems who was acting as a representative of the police and therefore a person in authority. But the real question was whether the fact that John Wray had taken the officers to the swamp where the rifle was located could be introduced into evidence before the jury. Without that evidence, there was nothing that linked John Wray to the rifle which had killed Donald Comrie.

In 1968, Canada had no rule which permitted a judge to refuse to admit evidence obtained by the authorities illegally or under circumstances which were unfair. Nevertheless after some serious hesitation, Mr. Justice

Henderson decided to exclude that evidence. As far as he was concerned, the methods employed by John Jurems and Inspector Lidstone to obtain that evidence were unfair and unjust to John Wray. He felt that if he admitted the evidence, it would bring the administration of justice into disrepute. He also knew that the evidence was crucial to the Crown's case. Unless it could be established that John Wray knew where the rifle had been hidden in the swamp, there was no evidence to link him to the killing. When Mr. Justice Henderson refused to admit the evidence, that was the end of the Crown's case against John Wray. Mr. Justice Henderson then directed the jury to aquit him and they did. The Crown appealed his ruling to the Ontario Court of Appeal. However, the Court of Appeal agreed with his ruling and dismissed the appeal.

The Crown then appealed to the Supreme Court of Canada and was successful. The Court was not prepared to accept that a trial judge had a broad general discretion to exclude any evidence which was relevant to the issues before the court. The common law had long recognized that evidence, no matter how illegally obtained, was still admissible against an accused so long as it was relevant to the issue before the court; and this was still the law of Canada. If trial judges were allowed to exclude evidence when they felt that the accused had been unfairly and unjustly treated, then there would be difficulty in achieving any sort of uniformity in the application of law. They disagreed with one of their members, Mr. Justice Spence who felt that it was the duty of every trial judge to guard against bringing the administration of justice into disrepute by excluding evidence obtained illegally by the police.

The Supreme Court of Canada ordered a new trial for John Wray. This time a new trial judge, Mr. Justice Haines, admitted into evidence the fact that John Wray had taken the police to the swamp where the rifle was located. Wray was found guilty by the jury of non-capital murder and was sentenced to life imprisonment.

## How The Exclusionary Rule Developed In The United States

The common law of England has never really concerned itself with the question of whether evidence has been obtained legally or illegally by the police. So long as the evidence has been relevant to an issue before the court, English courts have allowed it to be admitted. This does not mean that English judges have not been prepared to chastise police officers who have used unsavoury methods to gain evidence. They have done so on a number of occasions and usually in very strong language. But that has not prevented the court from admitting such evidence so long as it is pertinent to the question in issue and generally admissible under the rules of evidence. The English believe that police officers who commit unlawful acts or use unsavoury methods to obtain evidence should be subject to a civil law suit by the victim of their illegal conduct. This is still the law in England today.

In America, this view began to be rejected at the turn of this century. The United States, unlike Great Britain, had a written Constitution with certain fundamental guarantees to all its citizens. Constitutional guarantees were meaningless unless the courts were prepared to enforce them. To suggest that a person whose rights had been violated could seek redress in the civil courts ignored the realities of the situation. Most offenders are poor and have little reputation or standing in the community. Rarely will they have the funds necessary to hire a lawyer to sue the police. A civil law suit often takes longer than a criminal trial. At the time the civil law suit is ready to be heard, the accused might find himself in prison serving a sentence based on the evidence which he is now complaining was unlawfully obtained. People with criminal records hardly invite the sympathy of judges or juries against police officers. Even if they are successful, their position in the community is very unlikely to result in the award of any substantial damages.

However, the first Congress of the United States which drafted the first ten Amendments of the Constitution did not consider that it was necessary to give any specific authority to the courts to remedy a breach of the Constitution. It was expected that those whose duty it was to enforce the law would obey it. And so the old English common law rule was introduced and continued to prevail. Evidence obtained by illegal means was still admissible in a court of law. A person whose constitutional rights had been breached had to look for a remedy elsewhere.

However, in 1886, the Supreme Court decided that it could no longer avoid the issue. In *Boyd v. United States*, the Supreme Court was asked to decide whether a revenue law which required someone suspected of breaking that revenue law to produce his private papers and records was constitutionally valid. The prosecution needed the records and invoices of E.A. Boyd & Sons to prove its guilt. Boyd had produced the records but protested that the law had amounted to an unlawful search and seizure (Fourth Amendment) and a compulsion to incriminate himself (Fifth Amendment). Although the papers were incriminating, the Supreme Court refused to permit them to be admitted in evidence. Mr. Justice Bradley delivering the judgment of the court wrote:

> The principles laid down in this opinion affect the very essence of constitutional liberty and security . . . the sanctity of a man's home and the privacies of life . . . his indefeasible right of personal security, personal liberty and private property. . . .

Mr. Justice Bradley, however, was careful to limit the protection to private papers. The Fourth Amendment which protected "the right of people to be secure in their persons, houses, papers, and effects, against unreasonable searches and seizures . . ." could not prohibit the government from seizing and retaining contraband articles and stolen goods.

It was not until 28 years later that the Supreme Court of the United States decided to create an exclusionary rule which was applicable to all prosecutions in federal courts. It found it necessary to do so because other remedies were not successful in deterring government officials from carrying out unconstitutional searches and seizures. If the protections guaranteed by the Bill of Rights were to be respected, then some method had to be created to ensure that sanctions would be imposed upon those who violated them. The sanction was to prohibit the introduction into evidence of the item illegally seized. The landmark case was *Weeks v. United States* decided in 1914.

Freemont Weeks was charged with using the mails for an unlawful lotteries scheme. Federal officers had entered his home without a warrant and had searched and seized letters and correspondence without his consent. He applied to have the papers returned to him but his application was denied by the lower courts. However, Mr. Justice Day, speaking for the majority of the Supreme Court of the United States held that the lower courts were wrong:

> If letters and private documents can thus be seized and held and used in evidence against a citizen accused of an offense, the protection of the Fourth Amendment declaring his right to be secure against such searches and seizures, is of no value, and, so far as those thus placed are concerned, might as well be stricken from the Constitution. The efforts of the courts and their officials to bring the guilty to punishment, praiseworthy as they are, are not to be aided by the sacrifice of those great principles established by years of endeavour and suffering which have resulted in their embodiment in the fundamental law of the land.

However, the Court again was careful to limit its decision to searches conducted by federal officers resulting in federal prosecutions. State courts were not bound by the rule; but they could adopt the rule if they felt it was necessary to do so.

In 1949, an attempt was made to impose the exclusionary rule on state courts. In *Wolf v. Colorado*, the Supreme Court was now asked to decide whether the states were required by the due process clause of the Fourteenth Amendment to exclude evidence which would be inadmissible in a federal prosecution. The Fourteenth Amendment provided that no state was to "deprive any person of life, liberty, or property, *without due process of law.*" The Court, however, declined to do so.

Mr. Justice Frankfurter, writing for the majority, was satisfied that the Fourteenth Amendment did not subject criminal justice in the states to the constitutional protections of the first Ten Amendments. Furthermore, he did not feel that the exclusionary rule was "derived from the explicit requirements of the Fourth Amendment" but was rather "a matter of judicial implication."

How such arbitrary conduct should be checked, what remedies against it should be afforded, the means by which the right should be made effective, are all questions that are not to be so dogmatically answered as to preclude the varying solutions which spring from an allowable range of judgment on issues not susceptible of quantitative solution.

In other words, each state was required to ensure that every citizen was guaranteed protection against unreasonable search and seizure. But the exclusionary rule was not the only method by which a state could enforce the Fourth Amendment protection. If a state court concluded that other sanctions such as the criminal prosecution of the offending policeman or a civil action against him was an adequate protection, then that was satisfactory to the Supreme Court.

The three judges who dissented from this decision, however, were not satisfied that each state should be entitled to choose its own method to protect constitutional rights. This would only create different state standards. As far as they were concerned the criminal prosecution of policemen or a civil action against them was an illusory solution.

Mr. Justice Murphy summed up their concern in these words:

Imagination and zeal may invent a dozen methods to give content to the commands of the Fourth Amendment. But this court is limited to the remedies currently available. It cannot legislate the ideal system. If we would attempt the enforcement of the search and seizure clause in the ordinary case to date, we are limited to three devices: judicial exclusion of the illegally obtained evidence; criminal prosecution of violators; and civil action against violators in the action of trespass.

Alternatives are deceptive. The very statement conveys the impression that one possibility is as effective as the next. In this case their statement is blinding. For there is but one alternative to the rule of exclusion. That is no sanction at all. . . .

Little need be said concerning the possibilities of criminal prosecution. Self-scrutiny is a lofty ideal, but its exaltation reaches new heights if we expect a District Attorney to prosecute himself or his associates for well-meaning violations of the search and seizure clause during a raid the District Attorney or his associates have ordered. But there is an appealing ring in another alternative. A trespass action for damages is a venerable means of securing reparation for unauthorized invasion of the home. Why not put the old writ to a new use? When the Court cites cases permitting the action, the remedy seems complete.

But what an illusory remedy this is, if by "remedy" we mean a positive deterrent to police and prosecutors tempted to violate the Fourth Amendment. The appealing ring softens when we recall that in a trespass action the measure of damages is simply the extent of the injury to physical property. If the officer searches with care, he can avoid all but nominal damages — a penny, or a dollar. Are punitive damages possible? Perhaps. But a few states permit none, whatever the circumstances. In those that do, the plaintiff must show the real ill will or malice of the defendant, and surely it is not unreasonable to assume that one in honest pursuit of crime bears no malice towards the search victim. If that burden is carried, recovery may be defeated by the rule that there must be physical damages before punitive damages may be awarded. In addition, some states limit punitive damages to the actual expenses of litigation. . . . Even assuming the ill will of the officer, his reasonable grounds for belief that the home to be searched harbored evidence of crime is admissible in mitigation of punitive damages. . . . The bad reputation of the plaintiff is likewise admissible. If the evidence seized was actually used at a trial, that fact has been held a complete justification of the search, and a defence against the trespass action. . . . And even if the plaintiff hurdles all these obstacles, and gains a substantial verdict, the individual officer's finances may well make the judgment useless — for the municipality, of course, is not liable without its consent. Is it surprising that there is so little in the books concerning trespass actions for violation of the search and seizure clause?

The conclusion is inescapable that but one remedy exists to deter violations of the search and seizure clause. That is the rule which excludes illegally obtained evidence. Only by exclusion can we impress upon the zealous prosecutor that violation of the Constitution will do him no good. And only when that point is driven home can the prosecutor be expected to emphasize the importance of observing constitutional demands in his instructions to the police.

In 1949 when the Wolf case was before the trial courts, 47 states had considered the Weeks doctrine. Seventeen states had accepted it and thirty had rejected it. California had considered it in 1922 but rejected it. However, in 1955, the Supreme Court of California reversed itself and decided to adopt it in *People v. Cahan.* Its reason was that methods other than the exclusionary rule had failed to deter illegal police conduct. Mr. Justice Traynor for the Court declared:

We have been compelled to reach that conclusion because other remedies have completely failed to secure compliance with the constitutional provisions on the part of police officers with the attendant result that the courts under the old rule have been constantly required to participate in, and in effect condone, the lawless activities of law enforcement officers.

That decision, understandably, brought cries of outrage from law enforcement officers all over California. The District Attorney of Alameda County forecast that the,

net result of the exclusionary rule is that the persons who will benefit the most, in fact almost exclusively, are the blackmailer, the kidnapper, the big-time narcotic peddler, the racketeer, the dishonest gambler who preys in devious ways upon a gullible public, the panderer and procurer, the entrepreneur of syndicated prostitution, who, like the pimp, lives off the earnings of prostitutes, and other types of organized syndicated crime, such as, for example, the international conspiracy of communism to destroy the American way of life and the very constitutional rights which the majority opinion seeks to protect.

However, not all law enforcement officers agreed. Attorney General Edmund G. Brown, who subsequently became Governor of California noted two years later that,

The over-all effects of the Cahan decision, particularly in view of the rules now worked out by the Supreme Court, have been excellent. A much greater education is called for on the part of all peace officers of California. As a result, I am confident they will be much better police officers. I think there is more cooperation with the District Attorneys and this will make for better administration of criminal justice.

On June 19, 1961, the Supreme Court of the United States finally decided to overrule *Wolf v. Colorado* in the landmark decision, *Mapp v.*

*Ohio*. Dollree Mapp had been convicted of possession of obscene materials. Her home had been searched by the Cleveland police who were looking for a man suspected of bombing a house. During the course of the search, obscene pictures and books were found in her bedroom. The police, however, had no warrant to search the house. Ohio courts, under the authority of the Wolf decision, had decided to allow illegally obtained evidence to be admitted in a criminal prosecution. The Supreme Court decided that it was time to extend the exclusionary rule to all state courts. Mr. Justice Clark gave these reasons:

> ... in extending the substantive protections of due process to all constitutionally unreasonable searches — state or federal — it was logically and constitutionally necessary that the exclusion doctrine — an essential part of the right to privacy — be also insisted upon as an essential ingredient of the right newly recognized by the Wolf case. In short, the admission of the new constitutional right by Wolf could not consistently tolerate denial of its most important constitutional privilege, namely, the exclusion of the evidence which an accused had been forced to give by reason of the unlawful seizure. To hold otherwise is to grant the right but in reality to withhold its privilege and enjoyment. Only last year the Court itself recognized that the purpose of the exclusionary rule "is to deter — to compel respect for the constitutional guaranty in the only effectively available way — by removing the incentive to disregard it.

There was another reason why the rule should now apply to both federal and state courts:

> Moreover, our holding that [t]he exclusionary rule is an essential part of both the Fourth and the Fourteenth Amendments is not only the logical dictate of prior cases, but it also makes very good sense. There is no war between the Constitution and common sense. Presently, a federal prosecutor may make no use of evidence illegally seized, but a State's attorney across the street may, although he supposedly is operating under the enforceable prohibitions of the same Amendment. Thus the State, by admitting evidence unlawfully seized, serves to encourage disobedience to the Federal Constitution which it is bound to uphold.

To those who argued that the adoption of the rule would work to the benefit of criminals, he answered,

> There are those who say, as did Justice (then Judge) Cardozo, that under our constitutional exclusionary doctrine "the criminal is to go free because the constable has blundered". People v. Defore. In some cases this will undoubtedly be the result. But, as was said in Elkins, "there is another consideration — the imperative of judicial integrity". The criminal goes free, if he must, but it is the law that sets him free. Nothing can destroy a government more quickly than its failure to observe its own laws, or worse, its disregard of the charter of its own existence.

### Why did the Court decide to withdraw state option?

> The ignoble shortcut to conviction left open to the State tends to destroy the entire system of constitutional restraints on which the liberties of the people rest. Having once recognized that the right to privacy embodied in the Fourth Amendment is enforceable against the States, and that the right to be secure against rude invasions of privacy by

state officers is, therefore, constitutional in origin, we can no longer permit that right to remain an empty promise. Because it is enforceable in the same manner and to like effect as other basic rights secured by the Due Process Clause, we can no longer permit it to be revocable at the whim of any police officer who, in the name of law enforcement itself, chooses to suspend its enjoyment. Our decision, founded on reason and truth, gives to the individual no more than that which the Constitution guarantees him, to the police officer no less than that to which honest law enforcement is entitled, and, to the courts, that judicial integrity so necessary in the true administration of justice.

But *Mapp v. Ohio* did not end the criticism of the exclusionary rule. It has merely fuelled it and will continue to do so for some time. Recent decisions of the Supreme Court of the United States, under the leadership of Chief Justice Burger have started on a slow and deliberate retreat from an absolute exclusionary rule. In *United States v. Leon*, decided July 5, 1984, the Court accepted the argument that the exclusionary rule should be modified to permit the admission of evidence seized in reasonable good faith or in reliance on a search warrant which is later found to be defective. In the Leon case, a police officer had obtained a search warrant to search the home of a suspected drug trafficker. To obtain this warrant, the officer had to file an affidavit setting out the crucial facts supporting his belief that there were drugs in Leon's residence. Unfortunately, the information which the officer relied upon was over five months old.

The lower courts ruled that the information was "stale" and therefore insufficient to establish reasonable cause and excluded the evidence. But Mr. Justice White of the Supreme Court ruled that the evidence should have been admitted. It was his view that the exclusionary rule should "be more generally modified to permit the introduction of evidence obtained in the reasonable good faith belief that a search or seizure was in accord with the Fourth Amendment."

That view was followed in *Massachusetts v. Sheppard* also released on the same day. Sheppard was suspected of murdering his girlfriend, Sandra Boulware whose badly bruised body had been found in a vacant lot in the Rexbury section of Boston. To obtain a warrant to search Sheppard's residence, the investigating officer had filed an affidavit. The affidavit properly listed all of the items which the officer felt was important to the investigation. Unfortunately, the officer had used a form of affidavit generally used for a search of a controlled substance. This was compounded by the failure of the judge who was issuing the warrant to delete those portions of the warrant dealing with controlled drugs.

Once again Mr. Justice White ruled that the evidence should be admitted because there was "an objectively reasonable basis" for the officers' belief that they were searching pursuant to a valid warrant. As far as he was concerned, it was the judge, not the police officer, who had made the critical mistake. If the purpose of the exclusionary rule was to deter illegal police conduct, then it should not be applied in those circumstances where the officer acted in good faith.

# The Charter Creates An Exclusionary Rule In Canada

The Parliament of Canada undoubtedly had the American experience in mind when it drafted section 24 of the Charter of Rights and Freedoms. The Canadian Bill of Rights of 1960 had not provided sanctions for illegal police activity. This together with the fact that the Bill of Rights only applied to federal legislation made it a weak instrument for constitutional guarantee. In drafting the Charter, however, Parliament was careful to ensure that an exclusionary rule was not the only remedy available to someone whose rights and freedoms had been infringed. It also recognized that if there was to be an exclusionary rule, it had to be a compromise between those who wanted absolute sanctions upon illegal activity and those who wanted none at all.

> 24.(1) Anyone whose rights or freedoms, as guaranteed by this Charter, have been infringed or denied may apply to a court of competent jurisdiction to obtain such remedy as the court considers appropriate and just in the circumstances.
>
> (2) Where, in proceedings under subsection (1), a court concludes that evidence was obtained in a manner that infringed or denied any rights or freedoms guaranteed by this Charter, the evidence shall be excluded if it is established that, having regard to all the circumstances, the admission of it in the proceedings would bring the administration of justice into disrepute.

There is little doubt that the American critics of the exclusionary rule would welcome a provision such as section 24(1) in their Constitution. It empowers the court to grant such remedy as it "considers appropriate and just in the circumstances." This might involve an award of damages against a police officer personally, his immediate superior or even the municipality or government that employs him. It also means the right to order the police or the prosecution to return evidence illegally obtained to the owner. However, if the court is asked to exclude evidence from being presented by the prosecution, it is not required to do so automatically just because a person's constitutional rights have been infringed. That person must establish that if the evidence obtained as a result of the breach of his rights is admitted into the proceedings, it would bring the administration of justice into disrepute. Once he does this, the court is not entitled to refuse to exclude the evidence. Parliament was careful to use the imperative "shall" instead of the permissive "may." Judges are not entitled to pick and choose when they will exclude evidence. If it is established that there has been a denial of a right or freedom and, in all of the circumstances, it would bring the administration of justice into disrepute to admit the evidence into the proceedings, then the court must exclude it.

Shortly after the enactment of the Charter, Canadian courts were inundated with applications to exclude evidence because of a breach of a constitutional guarantee. Quite understandably, the courts approached section 24(2) with caution and restraint. Canadian courts have never felt that it has been necessary to curtail police activity, a problem which faced our neighbours to the south. That is not to say there have not been instances of overzealous police investigations. But as a whole, it has never really been an issue that has given the courts, or Canadian society, any great concern.

Initially, provincial appellate courts were quick to preach caution and restraint. They were careful to point out that the Charter was not intended to transform our legal system overnight. The breach of a fundamental right or freedom did not automatically bring about an exclusion of evidence. Illegal police activity had to be weighty and deliberate before it could be said that the administration of justice had been brought into disrepute. However, the courts were reluctant to give some definitive explanation as to the exact meaning of that expression.

Some courts have even reached back to authorities which preceded the Charter. In *Regina v. Rothman*, an undercover officer had been placed in the same cell as Rothman who had been arrested for possession of cannabis resin for the purpose of trafficking. Rothman initially suspected that the officer was a narcotics agent. In time, however, the officer was able to gain his confidence and Rothman made certain incriminating statements to him. Some members of the Supreme Court of Canada felt that there should be court intervention to exclude the statement because the conduct of the officer had brought the administration of justice into disrepute. They concluded that what would bring the administration of justice into disrepute was what would be prejudicial to the public interest in the integrity of the judicial process. Mr. Justice Lamer, however, suggested that to justify court intervention, the conduct itself must be so shocking as to cause the court to feel that it must dissociate itself from such conduct through the rejection of the evidence. He expressed his views in these words:

> There first must be a clear connection between the obtaining of the statement and the conduct; furthermore, that conduct must be so shocking as to justify the judicial branch of the criminal justice system in feeling that, short of dissociating itself from such conduct through rejection of the statement, its reputation and, as a result, that of the whole criminal justice system would be brought into disrepute.
> The judge, in determining whether under the circumstances the use of the statement in proceedings would bring the administration of justice into disrepute, should consider all of the circumstances of the proceedings, the manner in which the statement was obtained, the degree to which there was a breach of social values, the seriousness of the charge and the effect the exclusion would have on the result of the proceedings. It must also be borne in mind that the investigation of crime and the detection of criminals is not a game to be governed by the Marquess of Queensbury Rules. The authorities, in dealing with shrewd and often sophisticated criminals, must sometimes of necessity resort to tricks or other forms of deceit, and should not through the rule be hampered in their work. What should be repressed vigorously is conduct on their part that shocks the community.

The "shock the community" test was not a new concept. It had been suggested three decades earlier by Mr. Justice Frankfurter of the United States Supreme Court in *Wolf v. Colorado*. But section 24(2) does not speak of conduct that would "shock the community"; it speaks of conduct that would "bring the administration of justice into disrepute." In *Regina v. Simmons*, Chief Justice Howland of the Ontario Court of Appeal pointed out that there could be instances where the administration of justice was brought into disrepute "without necessarily shocking the Canadian community as a whole."

Furthermore, section 24(2) requires the court to consider all of the circumstances. This means that each case must be examined on its own particular merits. It means that the court is required to weigh and assess two competing values: on the one hand, the ascertainment of truth in the judicial process through the use of evidence, albeit illegally obtained; on the other hand, the protection and enforcement of constitutional rights and freedoms by the exclusion of that evidence. What must be considered, whenever section 24(2) is invoked, is whether the ascertainment of truth in the particular case must yield to a higher value — the integrity of the judicial process.

What are some of the factors which the court will consider? Here the courts have cautiously avoided any exhaustive identification of the relevant factors. Some of the factors suggested, however, have been — the nature and extent of the illegality — the unreasonableness of the conduct involved — was it committed in good faith, inadvertent or of a merely technical nature or was it deliberate, wilful or flagrant — was the breach motivated by urgency or the necessity to prevent loss or destruction of the evidence — how serious was the crime involved?

Predictability has always been recognized as the hallmark of an effective criminal law system. Unfortunately, an approach which weighs varying factors, unlike the definitive boundaries of an absolute exclusionary rule, will not contribute to consistent judicial determination. Nor can it be conducive to police restraint. On the other hand, one could hardly expect Canadian courts, only three years after the introduction of the Charter, to have developed a body of consistent precedent. American courts have had the luxury of over two centuries to resolve the issue and still the debate rages on.

In the next decade, the Canadian courts will have to decide whether police excesses can only be controlled by exclusion of evidence or whether the integrity of the judicial system can be protected by resorting to the potentially wide range of remedies available under section 24(1). In *Regina v. Duguay*, Mr. Justice Zuber expressed his concern that courts will exclude evidence almost automatically, because it will "inevitably lead us to a position very close to the exclusionary rule as it exists in the United States."

He stressed the importance of understanding,

> clearly what is being done when evidence is sought to be excluded pursuant to s. 24(2).
> Courts are being asked to suppress the truth. Most evidentiary rules of exclusion are
> based upon the lack of relevance, unreliability or the confusion that could be caused by
> admission. In the case of exclusion pursuant to s. 24(2), none of these frailties exists.

As far as he was concerned, respect for the integrity of the judicial process
should not be examined only through the eyes of the judiciary. The public
perception of our criminal law system is an equally relevant consideration.
He summed it up in these words:

> Frequent resort to the exclusion of evidence will create a perception by the public
> that the criminal justice system is a sort of legalistic game in which a misstep by the
> police confers immunity upon the accused. This perception will most certainly bring the
> administration of justice into disrepute.

# Appendix

## SCHEDULE B

# CONSTITUTION ACT, 1982

### PART I

### CANADIAN CHARTER OF RIGHTS AND FREEDOMS

Whereas Canada is founded upon principles that recognize the supremacy of God and the rule of law:

*Guarantee of Rights and Freedoms*

Rights and freedoms in Canada

1. The *Canadian Charter of Rights and Freedoms* guarantees the rights and freedoms set out in it subject only to such reasonable limits prescribed by law as can be demonstrably justified in a free and democratic society.

*Fundamental Freedoms*

Fundamental freedoms

2. Everyone has the following fundamental freedoms:

(*a*) freedom of conscience and religion;

(*b*) freedom of thought, belief, opinion and expression, including freedom of the press and other media of communication;

(*c*) freedom of peaceful assembly; and

(*d*) freedom of association.

*Democratic Rights*

Democratic rights of citizens

3. Every citizen of Canada has the right to vote in an election of members of the House of Commons or of a legislative assembly and to be qualified for membership therein.

Maximum duration of legislative bodies

4. (1) No House of Commons and no legislative assembly shall continue for longer than five years from the date fixed for the return of the writs at a general election of its members.

Continuation in special circumstances

(2) In time of real or apprehended war, invasion or insurrection, a House of Commons may be continued by Parliament and a legislative assembly may be continued by the legislature beyond five years if such continuation is not opposed by the votes of more than one-third of the members of the House of Commons or the legislative assembly, as the case may be.

Annual sitting of legislative bodies

5. There shall be a sitting of Parliament and of each legislature at least once every twelve months.

## Mobility Rights

Mobility of citizens

6. (1) Every citizen of Canada has the right to enter, remain in and leave Canada.

Rights to move and gain livelihood

(2) Every citizen of Canada and every person who has the status of a permanent resident of Canada has the right

(*a*) to move to and take up residence in any province; and

(*b*) to pursue the gaining of a livelihood in any province.

Limitation

(3) The rights specified in subsection (2) are subject to

(*a*) any laws or practices of general application in force in a province other than those that discriminate among persons primarily on the basis of province of present or previous residence; and

(*b*) any laws providing for reasonable residency requirements as a qualification for the receipt of publicly provided social services.

Affirmative action programs

(4) Subsections (2) and (3) do not preclude any law, program or activity that has as its object the amelioration in a province of conditions of individuals in that province who are socially or economically disadvantaged if the rate of employment in that province is below the rate of employment in Canada.

## *Legal Rights*

Life, liberty and security of person

7. Everyone has the right to life, liberty and security of the person and the right not to be deprived therof except in accordance with the principles of fundameñtal justice.

Search or seizure

8. Everyone has the right to be secure against unreasonable search or seizure.

Detention or imprisonment

9. Everyone has the right not to be arbitrarily detained or imprisoned.

Arrest or detention

10. Everyone has the right on arrest or detention

(*a*) to be informed promptly or the reasons therefor;

(*b*) to retain and instruct counsel without delay and to be informed of that right; and

(*c*) to have the validity of the detention determined by way of *habeas corpus* and to be released if the detention is not lawful.

Proceedings in criminal and penal matters

11. Any person charged with an offence has the right

(*a*) to be informed without unreasonable delay of the specific offence;

(*b*) to be tried within a reasonable time;

(*c*) not to be compelled to be a witness in proceedings against that person in respect of the offence;

(*d*) to be presumed innocent until proven guilty according to law in a fair and public hearing by an independent and impartial tribunal;

(*e*) not to be denied reasonable bail without just cause;

(*f*) except in the case of an offence under military law tried before a military tribunal, to the benefit of trial by jury where the maximum punishment for the offence is imprisonment for five years or a more severe punishment;

(*g*) not to be found guilty on account of any act or omission unless, at the time of the act or omission, it constituted an offence under Canadian or international law or was criminal according to the general principles of law recognized by the community of nations;

(*h*) if finally acquitted of the offence, not to be tried for it again and, if finally found guilty and punished for the offence, not to be tried or punished for it again; and

(*i*) if found guilty of the offence and if the punishment for the offence has been varied between the time of commission and the time of sentencing, to the benefit of the lesser punishment.

Treatment or punishment

12. Everyone has the right not to be subjected to any cruel and unusual treatment or punishment.

Self-crimination

13. A witness who testifies in any proceedings has the right not to have any incriminating evidence so given used to incriminate that witness in any other proceedings, except in a prosecution for perjury or for the giving of contradictory evidence.

Interpreter

14. A party or witness in any proceedings who does not understand or speak the language in which the proceedings are conducted or who is deaf has the right to the assistance of an interpreter.

## Equality Rights

Equality before and under law and equal protection and benefit of law

15. (1) Every individual is equal before and under the law and has the right to the equal protection and equal benefit of the law without discrimination and in particular, without discrimination based on race, national or ethnic origin, colour, religion, sex, age or mental or physical disability.

Affirmative action programs

(2) Subsection (1) does not preclude any law, program or activity that has as its object the amelioration of conditions of disadvantaged individuals or groups including those that are disad-

vantaged because of race, national or ethnic origin, colour, religion, sex, age or mental or physical disability.

## Official Languages of Canada

**Official languages of Canada**

16. (1) English and French are the official languages of Canada and have equality of status and equal rights and privileges as to their use in all institutions of the Parliament and government of Canada.

**Official languages of New Brunswick**

(2) English and French are the official languages of New Brunswick and have equality of status and equal rights and privileges as to their use in all institutions of the legislature and government of New Brunswick.

**Advancement of status and use**

(3) Nothing in this Charter limits the authority of Parliament or a legislature to advance the equality of status or use of English and French.

**Proceedings of Parliament**

17. (1) Everyone has the right to use English or French in any debates and other proceedings of Parliament.

**Proceedings of New Brunswick legislature**

(2) Everyone has the right to use English or French in any debates and other proceedings of the legislature of New Brunswick.

**Parliamentary statutes and records**

18. (1) The statutes, records and journals of Parliament shall be printed and published in English and French and both language versions are equally authoritative.

**New Brunswick statutes and records**

(2) The statutes, records and journals of the legislature of New Brunswick shall be printed and published in English and French and both language versions are equally authoritative.

**Proceedings in courts established by Parliament**

19. (1) Either English or French may be used by any person in, or in any pleading in or process issuing from, any court established by Parliament.

**Proceedings in New Brunswick courts**

(2) Either English or French may be used by any person in, or in any pleading in or process issuing from, any court of New Brunswick.

Communications
by public with
federal institutions

20. (1) Any member of the public in Canada has the right to communicate with, and to receive available services from, any head or central office of an institution of the Parliament or government of Canada in English or French, and has the same right with respect to any other office of any such institution where

(*a*) there is a significant demand for communications with and services from that office in such language; or

(*b*) due to the nature of the office, it is reasonable that communications with and services from that office be available in both English and French.

Communications
by public with
New Brunswick
institutions

(2) Any member of the public in New Brunswick has the right to communicate with, and to receive available services from, any office of an institution of the legislature or government of New Brunswick in English or French.

Continuation
of existing
constitutional
provisions

21. Nothing in sections 16 to 20 abrogates or derogates from any right, privilege or obligation with respect to the English and French languages, or either of them, that exists or is continued by virtue of any other provision of the Constitution of Canada.

Rights and
privileges
preserved

22. Nothing in sections 16 to 20 abrogates or derogates from any legal or customary right or privilege acquired or enjoyed either before or after the coming into force of this Charter with respect to any language that is not English or French.

*Minority Language Educational Rights*

Language of
instruction

23. (1) Citizens of Canada

(*a*) whose first language learned and still understood is that of the English or French linguistic minority population of the province in which they reside, or

(*b*) who have received their primary school instruction in Canada in English or French and reside in a province where the language in which they received that instruction is the language of the English or French linguistic minority population of the province,

have the right to have their children receive primary and secondary school instruction in that language in that province.

Continuity of language instruction

(2) Citizens of Canada of whom any child has received or is receiving primary or secondary school instruction in English or French in Canada, have the right to have all their children receive primary and secondary school instruction in the same language.

Application where numbers warrant

(3) The right of citizens of Canada under subsections (1) and (2) to have their children receive primary and secondary school instruction in the language of the English or French linguistic minority population of a province

(*a*) applies wherever in the province the number of children of citizens who have such a right is sufficient to warrant the provision to them out of public funds of minority language instruction, and

(*b*) includes, where the number of those children so warrants, the right to have them receive that instruction in minority language educational facilities provided out of public funds.

*Enforcement*

Enforcement of guaranteed rights and freedoms

24. (1) Anyone whose rights or freedoms, as guaranteed by this Charter, have been infringed or denied may apply to a court of competent jurisdiction to obtain such remedy as the court considers appropriate and just in the circumstances.

Exclusion of evidence bringing administration of justice into disrepute

(2) Where, in proceedings under subsection (1), a court concludes that evidence was obtained in a manner that infringed or denied any rights or freedoms guaranteed by this Charter, the evidence shall be excluded if it is established that, having

regard to all the circumstances, the admission of it in the proceedings would bring the administration of justice into disrepute.

## General

**Aboriginal rights and freedoms not affected by Charter**

25. The guarantee in this Charter of certain rights and freedoms shall not be construed so as to abrogate or derogate from any aboriginal, treaty or other rights or freedoms that pertain to the aboriginal peoples of Canada including

(*a*) any rights or freedoms that have been recognized by the Royal Proclamation of October 7, 1763; and

(*b*) any rights or freedoms that may be acquired by the aboriginal peoples of Canada by way of land claims settlement.

**Other rights and freedoms not affected by Charter**

26. The guarantee in this Charter of certain rights and freedoms shall not be construed as denying the existence of any other rights or freedoms that exist in Canada.

**Multicultural heritage**

27. This Charter shall be interpreted in a manner consistent with the preservation and enhancement of the multicultural heritage of Canadians.

**Rights guaranteed equally to both sexes**

28. Notwithstanding anything in this Charter, the rights and freedoms referred to in it are guaranteed equally to male and female persons.

**Rights respecting certain schools preserved**

29. Nothing in this Charter abrogates or derogates from any rights or privileges guaranteed by or under the Constitution of Canada in respect of denominational, separate or dissentient schools.

**Application to territories and territorial authorities**

30. A reference in this Charter to a province or to the legislative assembly or legislature of a province shall be deemed to include a reference to the Yukon Territory and the Northwest Territories, or to the appropriate legislative authority thereof, as the case may be.

**Legislative powers not extended**

31. Nothing in this Charter extends the legislative powers of any body or authority.

## Application of Charter

Application of
Charter

32. (1) This Charter applies

(*a*) to the Parliament and government of Canada in respect of all matters within the authority of Parliament including all matters relating to the Yukon Territory and Northwest Territories; and

(*b*) to the legislature and government of each province in respect of all matters within the authority of the legislature of each province.

Exception

(2) Notwithstanding subsection (1), section 15 shall not have effect until three years after this section comes into force.

Exception where
express declaration

33. (1) Parliament or the legislature of a province may expressly declare in an Act of Parliament or of the legislature, as the case may be, that the Act or a provision thereof shall operate notwithstanding a provision included in section 2 or sections 7 to 15 of this Charter.

Operation of
exception

(2) An Act or a provision of an Act in respect of which a declaration made under this section is in effect shall have such operation as it would have but for the provision of this Charter referred to in the declaration.

Five year
limitation

(3) A declaration made under subsection (1) shall cease to have effect five years after it comes into force or on such earlier date as may be specified in the declaration.

Re-enactment

(4) Parliament or a legislature of a province may re-enact a declaration made under subsection (1).

Five year
limitation

(5) Subsection (3) applies in respect of a re-enactment made under subsection (4).

## Citation

Citation

34. This Part may be cited as the *Canadian Charter of Rights and Freedoms*.

## Part VII

### General

Primacy of
Constitution of
Canada

**52.**—(1) The Constitution of Canada is the supreme law of Canada, and any law that is inconsistent with the provisions of the Constitution is, to the extent of the inconsistency, of no force or effect.

Constitution of
Canada

(2) The Constitution of Canada includes:

(*a*) the *Canada Act 1982*, including this Act;
(*b*) the Acts and orders referred to in the schedule; and
(*c*) any amendment to any Act or order referred to in paragraph (*a*) or (*b*).

Amendments to
Constitution of
Canada

(3) Amendments to the Constitution of Canada shall be made only in accordance with the authority contained in the Constitution of Canada.

# Notes

## Chapter 1: The Quest for a Canadian Charter of Rights and Freedoms

### Cases

*West Virginia State Bd. of Education v. Barnette*, 319 U.S. 624 (1943).
*Barron v. Mayor and City Council Baltimore*, 88 U.S. 15 (1833).
*Reference re Alberta Legislation*, [1938] S.C.R. 100 (the *Alberta Press Case*).
*Operation Dismantle Inc. v. The Queen* (1985), 18 D.L.R. (4th) 481 (S.C.C.).
*R. v. Big M Drug Mart Ltd.* (1985), 18 C.C.C. (3d) 385 (S.C.C.).

### Bibliography

Barth, Alan. *The Price of Liberty*. The Viking Press, 1963.
Friendly, Fred W. and Martha J.V. Elliott.*The Constitution — That Delicate Balance*. New York: Random House, 1984.
Hudon, Edward C. *Freedom of Speech and Press in America*. Washington D.C.: Public Affairs Press, 1963.
*From Sea Unto Sea*. Garden City, New York: W.G. Hardy Doubleday & Company Inc., 1959.
Creighton, Donald. *The Road to Confederation*. Toronto: Macmillan of Canada, 1964.
Tresolini, Rocco J. *These Liberties, Case Studies in Civil Rights*. Philadelphia: J.B. Lippincott Company, 1968.
Romanow, Ray, John Whyte, Howard Leeson. *Canada Notwithstanding, The Making of the Constitution 1976 - 1982*. Toronto: Carswell/Methuen, 1984.
Plucknett, Theodore. *A Concise History of the Common Law*, 5th ed. Toronto: Butterworth & Co., 1956.
Stephen, James Fitzjames. *A History of the Criminal Law of England*. 3 vols. London, 1883.
*The Federalist*. Modern Library Edition, 1941.
Mason, Alpheus Thomas. *The Supreme Court — Palladium of Freedom*. Ann Arbor: University of Michigan Press, 1962.
Stevens-Dodd, William Oliver. *Footsteps to Freedom*. New York: Mead & Co., 1963.

## Chapter 2: Freedom of Conscience and Religion

### Cases

*Saumur v. Quebec*, [1953] 2 S.C.R. 299.
*Roncarelli v. Duplessis*, [1959] S.C.R. 121.
*Chaput v. Romain*, [1955] S.C.R. 834.
*Minersville School Dist. v. Gobitis*, 310 U.S. 586 (1940).
*West Virginia State Bd. of Education v. Barnette*, 319 U.S. 624 (1943).
*McCollum v. Bd. of Education*, 333 U.S. 203 (1948).
*Zorach v. Clauson*, 343 U.S. 306 (1948).
*Engel v. Vitale*, 370 U.S. 421 (1962).
*Abbington School Dist. v. Schemp; Murray v. Curlett*, 374 U.S. 203 (1963).
*A.G. Ont. v. Hamilton Street Railway*, [1903] A.C. 524.
*Robertson and Rosetanni v. The Queen* (1964), 1 C.C.C. 1 (S.C.C.).
*Sherbert v. Verner*, 374 U.S. 398 (1963).
*R. v. Big M Drug Mart Ltd.* (1983), 9 C.C.C. (3d) 310 (Alta. C.A.); af-
    (1985) 18 C.C.C. (3d) 385 (S.C.C.).
*R. v. Videoflicks Ltd.* (1985), 15 C.C.C. 353 (Ont. C.A.).

### Bibliography

Tresolini, Rocco J. *These Liberties, Case Studies in Civil Rights.* Phila-
    delphia: J.B. Lippincott Company, 1968.
Friendly, Fred W. and Martha J. Elliott. *The Constitution — That
    Delicate Balance.* New York: Random House, 1984.
*The Canadian Charter of Rights and Freedoms: Commentary.* ed. Walter
    Tarnopolsky and Gerald A. Beaudoin. Toronto: Carswell Co. Ltd.,
    1982.
Pfeffer, Leo. *The Liberties of an American, The Supreme Court Speaks.*
    Boston: Beacon Press, 1963.
Krovitz, Milton R. *Religious Liberty and Conscience; A Constitutional
    Inquiry.* New York: Viking Press, 1968.

# Chapter 3: Freedom of Thought, Belief, Opinion and Expression

### Cases

*Terminello v. Chicago*, 337 U.S. 1 (1949).
*Schenk v. United States*, 249 U.S. 47 (1919).
*DeJonge v. Oregon*, 299 U.S. 353 (1937).
*Village of Skokie v. National Socialist Party of America*, 373 N.E. 21 (1978).
*Switzman v. Elbling*, [1957] S.C.R. 285.
*Boucher v. The Queen*, [1951] S.C.R. 265.
*R. v. Keegstra* (1985), 19 C.C.C. (3d) 254 (Alta. Q.B.).

### Bibliography

Hill, John Stuart. *Utilitarianism — Liberty — Representative Expression.* London, 1910.
de Beer, Gavin. *Charles Darwin.* London: Thomas Nelson (Printers) Ltd., 1963.
Plucknett, Theodore. *A Concise History of the Common Law.* Butterworth & Co. (Publishers) Ltd., 1956.
Weinberg, Arthur and Lila. *Clarence Darrow, A Sentimental Rebel.* New York: G.P. Putnam's Sons, 1980.
Stone, Irving. *Clarence Darrow for the Defense.* Garden City, New York: Doubleday & Co., 1941.
Tierney, Kevin. *Darrow — A Biography.* New York: Thomas Y. Crowell Publishers, 1979.
Stephen, James Fitzjames. *A History of the Criminal Law of England.* Vol. 2. London, 1883.
Tompkins, Jerry R., ed. *D-Days at Dayton — Reflections on the Scope Trial.* Baton Rouge: Louisiana State Univ. Press, 1965.
Hudon, Edward C. *Freedom of Speech and Press in America.* Washington, D.C.: Public Affairs Press, 1963.

## Chapter 4: Freedom of the Press and other Media of Expression

### Cases

*R. v. Shipley* (1784), 4 Doug. 73, 99 E.R. 774.
*R. v. Zenger* (1735), 17 Howell's State Trials 675.
*R. v. Cuthill* (1799), 27 Howell's State Trials 674.
*De Libellis Famosis* (1606), 3 Co. Rep. 254, 77 E.R. 250.
*Schaefer v. United States*, 251 U.S. 466 (1920).
*Near v. Minnesota*, 283 U.S. 697 (1931).
*Grosjean v. American Press Co.*, 297 U.S. 233 (1936).
*Reference re Alberta Legislation*, [1938] S.C.R. 100.
*R. v. Oakes* (1983), 2 C.C.C. (3d) 339 (Ont. C.A.); leave to appeal to S.C.C.
   granted March 21, 1983.

### Bibliography

Hudon, Edward C. *Freedom of Speech and Press in America*. Public
   Affairs Press, 1963.
Friendly, Fred W. and Martha J.H. Elliott. *The Constitution — That
   Delicate Balance*. Random House, 1984.
Stephen, James Fitzjames. *A History of the Criminal Law of England*,
   Vol. 3. London, 1883.
Stryker, Lloyd Paul. *For the Defense — Thomas Erskine*. New York, 1947.
Law Reform Commission of Canada. *Defamatory Libel*. Working Paper
   35, 1984.

# Chapter 5: Freedom From Arbitrary Detention or Imprisonment

## Cases

*Hirabayashi v. United States*, 320 U.S. 81 (1943).
*Korematsu v. United States*, 323 U.S. 193 (1944).
*Ex parte Endo*, 323 U.S. 308 (1944).

## Bibliography

Haggart, Ron and Aubrey E. Golden. *Rumours of War.* New Press, 1971.
Adachi, Ken. *The Enemy that Never Was — A History of the Japanese Canadians.* McClelland & Stewart, 1976.
Gwyn, Richard. *The Northern Magus.* McClelland & Stewart, 1980.
Berger, Thomas R. *Fragile Freedoms, Human Rights & Dissent in Canada.* Clark, Irwin & Co. Ltd., 1981.
Schwartz, Bernard. *Super Chief, Earl Warren and His Supreme Court — A Judicial Biography.* New York & London: New York University Press, 1983.

# Chapter 6: Freedom From Unreasonable Search and Seizure

## Cases

*Wilkes v. Lord Halifax* (1765), State Tr. 1406.
*Entick v. Carrington* (1765), 19 State Tr. 1029, 95 E.R. 807.
*Boyd v. United States*, 116 U.S. 616 (1885).
*Harris v. United States*, 331 U.S. 145 (1947).
*R. v. L.A.R.* (1983), 9 C.C.C. (3d) 144 (Man. Q.B.).
*R. v. Altseimeir* (1982), 1 C.C.C. (3d) 7 (Ont. C.A.).
*R. v. Rao* (1984), 12 C.C.C. (3d) 97 (Ont. C.A.).
*Hunter v. Southam Inc.* (1984), 14 C.C.C. (3d) 97 (S.C.C.).
*R. v. Collins* (1983), 5 C.C.C. (3d) 141 (B.C.C.A.).

## Bibliography

Kronenberger, Louis. *The Extraordinary Mr. Wilkes: His Life and Times.* Garden City, New York: Doubleday & Co., 1974.
Barth, Alan. *The Price of Liberty.* New York: Viking Press, 1961.
Alden, John R. *A History of the American Revolution.* New York: Alfred A. Knopf, 1975.
Tresolini, Rocco J. *These Liberties, Case Studies in Civil Rights.* Philadelphia: J.B. Lippincott Co., 1968.

## Chapter 7: The Right to Habeas Corpus

### Cases

*Sommersett Case* (1772), 20 State Tr. 1.
*Darnel's Case* (1627), 3 St. Tr. 1.

### Bibliography

Higgins, Nathan Irvin. *Black Odyssey — The Afro-American Ordeal in Slavery*. New York: Pantheon Books, 1977.
Woodson, Carter C. *The Negro in Our History*. Washington, D.C.: The Associated Publishers Inc., 1922.
Watson, J. Steven. *The Reign of George III; 1760 - 1815*. Oxford: Clarendon Press, 1960.

## Chapter 8: The Right to Remain Silent

### Cases

*Lilburne* (1637), 3 State Tr. 1316.
*Escobedo v. Illinois*, 378 U.S. 478 (1964).
*Miranda v. Arizona*, 384 U.S. 436 (1966).
*R. v. Marcoux and Solomon* (1976), 24 C.C.C. (2d) 1 (S.C.C.).

### Bibliography

Salhany, Roger E. and Robert J. Carter, ed. *Studies in Canadian Criminal Evidence*. Toronto: Butterworth's, 1972.
Ratushny, Ed. *Self-Incrimination in the Canadian Criminal Process*. Toronto: Carswell Co. Ltd., 1979.
Stephen, James Fitzjames. *History of the Criminal Law in England*. 3 vols. London, 1883.
Griswold, Erwin. *The Fifth Amendment To-day*.. Cambridge, Mass., 1955.
*Wigmore on Evidence*. Vol. 8, Mcnaughton rev. 1961.
Levy, Leonard W. *Origins of the Fifth Amendment*. New York: Oxford University Press, 1968.
Meltzer, Milton. *Right to Remain Silent*. New York: Harcourt Brace Jovanovich, 1972.
"Abe Fortas, The Fifth Amendment To-day: Nemo Tenetur Prodere Seipsum," (1954), 25 Clev. B.A.J. 91.

## Chapter 9: Trial By Jury

### Cases

*Bushell's Case* (1670), Vaughan 135, 89 E.R. 2.
*Throckmortons Case* (1554), State Tr. 869.
*R. v. Shipley* (1784), 4 Doug. 73.
*R. v. Crate* (1983), 7 C.C.C. (3d) 127 (Alta. C.A.).
*R. v. Bryant* (1985), 16 C.C.C. (3d) 408 (Ont. C.A.).

### Bibliography

Devlin, Sir Patrick. *Trial by Jury.* London: Stevens & Sons, 1966.
Williams, Glanville. *The Proof of Guilt.* 3rd ed. London: Stevens & Sons, 1963.
Blackstone, Sir William. *Commentaries on the Laws of England.* 4 vols.
Peare, Catherine. *William Penn.* Philadelphia & New York: J.B. Lippincott Co., 1957.
Thayer. *Preliminary Treatise on Evidence.* London, 1898.
Stephen, James Fitzjames. *A History of the Criminal Law of England.* 3 vols. London, 1883.
Hardwick, Michael. *The Verdict of the Court.* London, 1960.
Moore, Lloyd E. *Tools of Kings, Palladium of Justice.* Cincinnati: W.H. Anderson Co., 1973.

## Chapter 10: The Right to Counsel

### Cases

*United States v. Murphy*, 222 F. (2d) 698 (1955).
*Gideon v. Wainwright*, 372 U.S. 335 (1963).
*Powell v. Alabama*, 287 U.S. 45 (1932).
*Escobedo v. Illinois*, 378 U.S. 478 (1964).
*Miranda v. Arizona*, 384 U.S. 446 (1966).
*R. v. Brownridge* (1972), 7 C.C.C. (2d) 417 (S.C.C.).
*R. v. Chromiak* (1979), 49 C.C.C. (2d) 217 (S.C.C.).
*R. v. Therens* (1983), 5 C.C.C. (3d) 409 (Sask. C.A.); affirmed (1985)
    18 C.C.C. (3d) 481 (S.C.C.).
*R. v. Talbourdet* (1984), 12 C.C.C. (3d) 173 (Sask. C.A.).
*R. v. Ahearn* (1983), 8 C.C.C. (3d) 257 (P.E.I.S.C.).
*R. v. Anderson* (1984), 10 C.C.C. (3d) 417 (Ont. C.A.).
*R. v. Manninen* (1984), 8 C.C.C. (3d) 193 (Ont. C.A.).

### Bibliography

Lewis, Anthony. *Gideon's Trumpet*. New York: Random House, 1964.
Hall, Livingston and Yale Kasimar. *Modern Criminal Procedure*. St.
    Paul, Minn.: West Publishing Co., 1966.
Williams, Glanville. *The Proof of Guilt*, 3rd ed. London: Stevens & Sons,
    1963.

# Chapter 11: Remedying the Breach

## Cases

*R. v. Wray*, [1970] 3 C.C.C. 122 (Ont. C.A.); reversed [1970] 4 C.C.C. 1 (S.C.C.). Transcript of evidence from Robert J. Carter, Q.C., counsel for accused.

*Boyd v. United States*, 116 U.S. 616 (1885).

*Weeks v. United States*, 232 U.S. 383 (1914).

*Wolf v. Colorado*, 338 U.S. 25 (1949).

*People v. Cahan*, 44 Cal. 2d 434 (1955).

*Mapp v. Ohio*, 367 U.S. 643 (1951).

*United States v. Leon*, 104 S. Ct. 3405 (1984).

*Massachusetts v. Sheppard*, 104 S. Ct. 3424 (1984).

*R. v. Rothman* (1981), 20 C.R. (3d) 97 (S.C.C.).

*R. v. Simmons* (1984), 11 C.C.C. (3d) 192 (Ont. C.A.).

*R. v. Duguay* (1985), 18 C.C.C. (3d) 289 (Ont. C.A.).

## Bibliography

Barth, Alan. *The Price of Liberty.* New York: Viking Press, 1961.

Bernstein, Sidney. "Supreme Court Review." *Trial Magazine* (September 1984).

Hall, Livingston and Yale Kasimar. *Modern Criminal Procedure.* St. Paul, Minn.: West Publishing Co., 1966.

# Index